FREE VIDEO  FREE VIDEO

Essential Test Tips Video from Trivium Test Prep!

Dear Customer,

Thank you for purchasing from Trivium Test Prep! We're honored to help you prepare for your exam.

To show our appreciation, we're offering a **FREE *Essential Test Tips* Video by Trivium Test Prep**.* Our video includes 35 test preparation strategies that will make you successful on your exam. All we ask is that you email us your feedback and describe your experience with our product. Amazing, awful, or just so-so: we want to hear what you have to say!

To receive your **FREE *Essential Test Tips* Video**, please email us at 5star@triviumtestprep.com. Include "Free 5 Star" in the subject line and the following information in your email:

1. The title of the product you purchased.
2. Your rating from 1 – 5 (with 5 being the best).
3. Your feedback about the product, including how our materials helped you meet your goals and ways in which we can improve our products.
4. Your full name and shipping address so we can send your **FREE *Essential Test Tips* Video**.

If you have any questions or concerns please feel free to contact us directly at: 5star@triviumtestprep.com.

Thank you!

– Trivium Test Prep Team

*To get access to the free video please email us at 5star@triviumtestprep.com, and please follow the instructions above.

TOEFL Preparation Book 2022-2023:

STUDY GUIDE WITH PRACTICE TEST QUESTIONS
(READING, LISTENING, SPEAKING, AND WRITING)
FOR THE TOEFL IBT EXAM

ELISSA SIMON

TABLE OF CONTENTS

INTRODUCTION

Congratulations on choosing to take the Test of English as a Foreign Language (TOEFL)! By purchasing this book, you've taken an important step toward your academic career in the English-speaking world.

This guide will provide you with a detailed overview of the TOEFL so that you know exactly what to expect on test day. We'll take you through all the concepts covered on the assessments and give you the opportunity to test your knowledge with practice questions. Even if it's been a while since you last took a major exam, don't worry; we'll make sure you're more than ready!

WHAT IS THE TOEFL?

The TOEFL measures a candidate's English-language ability for advanced academic study. It tests and affirms English reading, writing, speaking, and listening abilities at the undergraduate and postgraduate levels.

WHAT'S ON THE TOEFL?

The exam includes four sections: Listening, Reading, Writing, and Speaking. Because the TOEFL tests your ability to communicate using these combined skills, you must take all sections of the test on the same day.

What's on the TOEFL?

TEST	TOPICS	NUMBER OF QUESTIONS	TIME
Reading	■ three or four articles or excerpts from books, magazines, or newspapers on academic topics of general interest at the undergraduate level (total text length is 2,150 – 2,750 words) ■ Each passage is followed by multiple-choice questions to test for comprehension.	30 – 40	54 – 72 minutes
Listening	■ a conversation in a social context ■ one or two lectures on an academic topic ■ Each recording is followed by multiple-choice questions to test for comprehension.	28 – 39	41 – 57 minutes

10-MINUTE BREAK

TEST	TOPICS	NUMBER OF QUESTIONS	TIME
Speaking	■ Task 1: Express an opinion on a familiar topic. ■ Task 2: Read a text and listen to part of a lecture or conversation on an academic or campus-related topic; speak about these. ■ Task 3: Summarize the main points of the text and lecture. ■ Task 4: Listen to and summarize part of a lecture on an academic topic.	4 tasks	17 minutes
Writing	■ Task 1: Write an essay summarizing a text and lecture on an academic topic. ■ Task 2: Write an essay expressing your opinion on an issue.	2 tasks	50 minutes
Total		approximately 80 multiple choice, 2 essays, and 4 speaking tasks	approximately 3 ½ hours (includes check-in time)

HOW IS THE TOEFL SCORED?

For the multiple-choice portion of the test, you will receive one point for each question you answer correctly. Those raw scores will be converted to a scaled score of 0 – 30.

On the Speaking section, each of the four tasks is rated from 0 – 4. Those scores are added together and scaled to a score of 0 – 30.

On the Writing section, each of the two tasks is rated from 0 – 5. As on the other sections of the test, those scores are added up and scaled from 0 – 30.

Ultimately, you will have four scaled scores from 0 – 30 (one for each section of the test—Reading, Listening, Speaking, and Writing). The scaled scores combine to a total score of 0 – 120.

Speaking scores are based on clarity, fluidity, and correct pronunciation and intonation. A strong response will show good use of grammar, complex structures, and advanced vocabulary.

Writing scores are likewise based on clarity. A strong response will demonstrate a well-structured essay that adequately responds to the questions using complex sentences, coherence, a variety of vocabulary, and appropriate grammar and syntax. A few minor grammatical or mechanical errors may occur.

You cannot pass or fail the TOEFL. Your scores are a reflection of your proficiency in English. The institution or school to which you are sending your scores will have a score requirement. Check with the school or institution to which you are applying for details. TOEFL scores are valid for two years from the date of testing.

How is the TOEFL Administered?

The TOEFL is offered over fifty times a year at test centers worldwide. Create an Educational Testing Service (ETS) account to find available test centers and dates and to register for an exam at https://www.ets.org/toefl/ibt/register/centers_dates/.

On test day, arrive early. Check with the facility and ielts.org to make sure you know what type of identification to bring. Original copies of government-issued photo identification are usually required. Check https://www.ets.org/toefl/ibt/register/id/ for the most up-to-date information. Personal belongings, cell phones, and other electronic, photographic, recording, or listening devices are not permitted in the testing center. Many testing centers offer lockers to secure your personal items, but you should check with the facility beforehand to find out if storage is available.

About this Guide

This guide will help you master the most important test topics and develop critical test-taking skills. We have built features into our books to prepare you for your exams and increase your score. Along with a detailed summary of the test's format, content, and scoring, we offer an in-depth overview of the content knowledge required to score high on your TOEFL. In the review, you'll find sidebars that provide interesting information, highlight key concepts, and review content so that you can solidify your understanding of important concepts. You can also test your knowledge with sample questions throughout the text and with practice questions. We're pleased you've chosen Trivium to be a part of your journey!

READING

The reading questions on the TOEFL focus on **ACADEMIC READING**. The Academic Reading section has three or four passages, each followed by nine or ten questions. The texts will address issues of general knowledge. They are taken from articles, books, and journals. You do not need any background knowledge to answer the questions beyond what is provided in the readings. You may need to interpret visual images like diagrams or graphs.

Questions may address anything from the main idea of the passage, vocabulary words in the passage, the author's message or intention, and more. Questions are mostly multiple choice, but may include sentence completion, identifying information in the text, or other formats.

This chapter will review key concepts in reading comprehension to help you prepare for the exam.

THE MAIN IDEA

The **TOPIC** is a word or short phrase that explains what a passage is about. The **MAIN IDEA** is a complete sentence that explains what the author is trying to say about the topic. Generally, the **TOPIC SENTENCE** is the first (or near the first) sentence in a paragraph. It is a general statement that introduces the topic so that the reader knows what to expect.

The **SUMMARY SENTENCE**, on the other hand, frequently (but not always!) comes at the end of a paragraph or passage because it wraps up all the ideas presented. This sentence summarizes what an author has said about the topic. Some passages, particularly short ones, will not include a summary sentence.

> ✔ To find the main idea, identify the topic and then ask, "What is the author trying to tell me about the topic?"

Table 1.1. Identifying the Topic and Main Idea

The cisco, a foot-long freshwater fish native to the Great Lakes, once thrived throughout the basin but had virtually disappeared by the 1950s. However, today fishermen are pulling them up by the net-load in Lake Michigan and Lake Ontario. It is highly unusual for a native species to revive, and the reason for the cisco's reemergence is even more unlikely. The cisco have an invasive species—quagga mussels—to thank for their return. Quagga mussels depleted nutrients in the lakes, harming other species highly dependent on these nutrients. Cisco, however, thrive in low-nutrient environments. As other species—many of which were invasive—diminished, cisco flourished in their place.

TOPIC SENTENCE	The cisco, a foot-long freshwater fish native to the Great Lakes, once thrived throughout the basin but had virtually disappeared by the 1950s.
TOPIC	cisco
SUMMARY SENTENCE	As other species—many of which were invasive—diminished, cisco flourished in their place.
MAIN IDEA	Cisco had nearly disappeared from the lake but now flourish thanks to the invasive quagga mussel.

Practice Questions

1. Tourists flock to Yellowstone National Park each year to view the geysers that bubble and erupt throughout it. What most of these tourists do not know is that these geysers are formed by a caldera—a hot crater in the earth's crust—which was created by a series of three eruptions of an ancient super volcano. These eruptions, which began 2.1 million years ago, spewed between 1,000 and 2,450 cubic kilometers of volcanic matter at such a rate that the volcano's magma chamber collapsed, creating the craters.

   What is the topic of the passage?

   A) tourists

   B) geysers

   C) volcanic eruptions

   D) super volcanos

2. The Battle of Little Bighorn, commonly called Custer's Last Stand, was a battle between the Lakota, the Northern Cheyenne, the Arapaho, and the Seventh Cavalry Regiment of the US Army. Led by war leaders Crazy Horse and Chief Gall and the religious leader Sitting Bull, the allied tribes of the Plains Indians decisively defeated their US foes. Two hundred and sixty-eight US soldiers were killed, including General George Armstrong Custer, two of his brothers, his nephew, his brother-in-law, and six Indian scouts.

   What is the main idea of this passage?

   A) Most of General Custer's family died in the Battle of Little Bighorn.

   B) The Seventh Cavalry regiment was formed to fight Native American tribes.

   C) Sitting Bull and George Custer were fierce enemies.

   D) The Battle of Little Bighorn was a significant victory for the Plains Indians.

SUPPORTING DETAILS

Statements that describe or explain the main idea are SUPPORTING DETAILS. Supporting details are often found after the topic sentence. They support the main idea through examples, descriptions, and explanations.

Authors may add details to support their argument or claim. FACTS are details that point to truths, while OPINIONS are based on personal beliefs or judgments. To differentiate between fact and opinion, look for statements that express feelings, attitudes, or beliefs that can't be proven (opinions) and statements that can be proven (facts).

> ⚠ To find supporting details, look for sentences that connect to the main idea and tell more about it.

Table 1.2. Supporting Details and Fact and Opinion

Bait is an important element of fishing. Some people use live bait, such as worms and night crawlers. Others use artificial bait, such as lures and spinners. Live bait has a scent that fish are drawn to. Live bait is a good choice for fishing. It's cheap and easy to find. Lures can vibrate, make noise, and mimic the movements of some fish. People should choose artificial bait over live bait because it can be used multiple times.

SUPPORTING DETAILS	Lures can vibrate, make noise, and mimic the movements of some fish.
FACT	Live bait has a scent that fish are drawn to.
OPINION	Live bait is a good choice for fishing.

Practice Questions

3. Increasingly, companies are turning to subcontracting services rather than hiring full-time employees. This provides companies with advantages like greater flexibility, reduced legal responsibility to employees, and lower possibility of unionization within the company. However, this has led to increasing confusion and uncertainty over the legal definition of employment. Courts have grappled with questions about the hiring company's responsibility in maintaining fair labor practices. Companies argue that they delegate that authority to subcontractors, while unions and other worker-advocate groups argue that companies still have a legal obligation to the workers who contribute to their business.

   Which detail BEST supports the idea that using contract employees is beneficial to companies?

   A) Uncertainty over the legal definition of employment increases.

   B) Companies still have a legal obligation to contractors.

   C) There is a lower possibility of unionization within the company.

   D) Contractors, not companies, control fair labor practices.

4. Chalk is a colorful way for kids and adults to have fun and be creative. Chalk is used on playgrounds and sidewalks. Children love to draw pictures in different colors. The designs are beautiful, but they are also messy. Chalk doesn't clean up easily. It has to wash away. Chalk is also used by cafés and bakeries. Shops use chalk to showcase their menus and special items. It is a great way to advertise their food.

Which statement from the passage is an opinion?

A) It is a great way to advertise their food.

B) Chalk doesn't clean up easily.

C) It has to wash away.

D) Shops use chalk to showcase their menus and special items.

DRAWING CONCLUSIONS

Look for facts, character actions and dialogue, how each sentence connects to the topic, and the author's reasoning for an argument when drawing conclusions.

Readers can use information that is EXPLICIT, or clearly stated, along with information that is IMPLICIT, or indirect, to make inferences and DRAW CONCLUSIONS. Readers can determine meaning from what is implied by using details, context clues, and prior knowledge. When answering questions, consider what is known from personal experiences and make note of all information the author has provided before drawing a conclusion.

Table 1.3. Drawing Conclusions

When the Spanish-American War broke out in 1898, the US Army was small and understaffed. President William McKinley called for 1,250 volunteers to serve in the First US Volunteer Calvary. The ranks were quickly filled by cowboys, gold prospectors, hunters, gamblers, Native Americans, veterans, police officers, and college students looking for an adventure. The officer corps was composed of veterans of previous wars. With more volunteers than it could accept, the army set high standards: all the recruits had to be skilled on horseback and with guns. Consequently, they became known as the Rough Riders.

QUESTION	Why are the volunteers named Rough Riders?
EXPLICIT INFORMATION	Different people volunteered, men were looking for adventure, and recruits had to be extremely skilled on horseback and with guns due to a glut of volunteers.
IMPLICIT INFORMATION	Men had previous occupations, officer corps veterans worked with volunteers.
CONCLUSION DRAWN	The men were called Rough Riders because they were inexperienced yet particularly enthusiastic to help with the war and were willing to put in extra effort to join.

Practice Question

5. After World War I, political and social forces pushed for a return to normalcy in the United States. The result was disengagement from the larger world and increased focus on American economic growth and personal enjoyment. Caught in the middle were American writers, raised on the values of the prewar world and frustrated with what they viewed as the superficiality and materialism of postwar American culture. Many of them fled to Paris, where they became known as the "lost generation," creating a trove of literary works criticizing their home culture and delving into their own feelings of alienation.

Which conclusion about the effects of war is most likely true?

A) War served as an inspiration for literary works.

B) It was difficult to stabilize countries after war occurred.

C) Writers were torn between supporting war and their own ideals.

D) Individual responsibility and global awareness declined after the war.

THE AUTHOR'S PURPOSE AND POINT OF VIEW

The AUTHOR'S PURPOSE is an author's reason for writing a text. Authors may write to share an experience, entertain, persuade, or inform readers. This can be done through persuasive, expository, and narrative writing.

PERSUASIVE WRITING influences the actions and thoughts of readers. Authors state an opinion, then provide reasons that support the opinion. EXPOSITORY WRITING outlines and explains steps in a process. Authors focus on a sequence of events. NARRATIVE WRITING tells a story. Authors include a setting, plot, characters, problem, and solution in the text.

Authors also share their POINT OF VIEW (perspectives, attitudes, and beliefs) with readers. Identify the author's point of view by word choice, details, descriptions, and characters' actions. The author's attitude or TONE can be found in word choice that conveys feelings or stance on a topic.

> Use the acronym P.I.E.S.— *persuade*, *inform*, *entertain*, *state*—to help you remember elements of an author's purpose.

TEXT STRUCTURE is the way the author organizes a text. A text can be organized to show a problem and solution, compare and contrast, or even investigate cause and effect. Structure of a text can give insight into an author's purpose and point of view. If a text is organized to pose an argument or advertise a product, it can be considered persuasive. The author's point of view will be revealed in how thoughts and opinions are expressed in the text.

Table 1.4. The Author's Purpose and Point of View

Superfoods are foods that are found in nature. They are rich in nutrients and low in calories. Many people are concerned about healthy diets and weight loss, so superfoods are a great meal choice! The antioxidants and vitamins found in superfoods decrease the risk of diseases and aid in heart health.

AUTHOR'S PURPOSE	persuade readers of the benefit of superfoods
POINT OF VIEW	advocates superfoods as "a great meal choice"
TONE	positive, encouraging, pointing out the benefits of superfoods, using positive words like *great* and *rich*
STRUCTURE	cause and effect to show the results of eating superfoods

Practice Questions

6. University of California, Berkeley researchers decided to tackle an age-old problem: why shoelaces come untied. They recorded the shoelaces of a volunteer walking on a treadmill by attaching devices to record the acceleration, or g-force, experienced by the knot. The results were surprising. A shoelace knot experiences more g-force from a person walking than any rollercoaster can generate. However, if the person simply stomped or swung their feet—the two movements that make up a walker's stride—the g-force was not enough to undo the knots.

    What is the purpose of this passage?

    A) to confirm if shoelaces always come undone

    B) to compare the force of treadmills and rollercoasters

    C) to persuade readers to tie their shoes tighter

    D) to describe the results of an experiment on shoelaces

7. What do you do with plastic bottles? Do you throw them away, or do you recycle or reuse them? As landfills continue to fill up, there will eventually be no place to put our trash. If you recycle or reuse bottles, you will help reduce waste and turn something old into a creative masterpiece!

Which of the following BEST describes what the author believes?

A) Landfills are unnecessary.

B) Reusing objects requires creativity.

C) Recycling helps the environment.

D) Reusing objects is better than recycling.

8. Negative cinematic representations of gorillas have provoked fear and contribute to hunting practices that endanger gorilla populations. It's a shame that many films portray them as scary and aggressive creatures. Their size and features should not be cause for alarm. Gorillas are actually shy and act aggressively only when provoked.

What can be inferred about the author's attitude toward gorillas?

A) The author is surprised that people do not know the truth about gorillas.

B) The author is concerned that movies distort people's opinion of gorillas.

C) The author is saddened by the decrease in gorilla populations.

D) The author is afraid that gorillas are being provoked.

9.

Want smoother skin? Try Face Lace, a mix of shea butter and coconut oil. Like most creams it is soft and easy to apply. We rank #1 in sales and free trials. Our competitor Smooth Moves may be great for blemishes, but we excel at reducing the signs of aging!

What is the structure of this text?

A) cause and effect

B) order and sequence

C) problem and solution

D) compare and contrast

TEXT FEATURES

TEXT FEATURES are components of a text that include information that is not in the main text. They help readers determine what is essential in a text and show where to find key information. Before reading, look at the text features to get an understanding of what a text is about.

Text features help readers increase background knowledge and learn new information.

HEADINGS and SUBHEADINGS show how information is organized and help readers identify the main points of each section in a text.

FOOTNOTES are notes at the bottom of a page that reference or cite information, definitions, explanations, or comments.

Text features such as ITALICS and BOLDFACE are used for emphasis. Italicized words appear slanted and signify titles, scientific terms, footnote references, and emphasized words. Boldface print makes words stand out from the rest of the text on a page and draws the reader's attention. It is used to highlight ideas, introduce new vocabulary, or emphasize main points.

The TABLE OF CONTENTS and INDEX are text features that help organize information. The table of contents shows a book's structure, outlining its sections and chapters. An index consists of a list of words and phrases in alphabetical order that outlines various topics in a book. Page numbers are provided to guide readers to sections of the book.

Table 1.5. Text Features

CHAPTER TWO: RATTLESNAKES

Rattlesnake Habitats

There are 13 species (*crotalus* or *sistrurus*) of rattlesnakes. Rattlesnakes adapt to different **habitats**. They can live in deserts, meadows, or swamps. Rocky crevices are great places to hide and make dens.

Keeping Predators Away

Rattlesnakes have a rattle at the base of their tails. The vibrations of the rattle deter **predators**. Hissing sounds are also a warning to other animals. Other ways to ward off predators include coiling their bodies and raising their heads in order to strike and bite.[1]

---
[1] Some rattlesnakes camouflage themselves to avoid predators.

BOLDING	habitats, predators
ITALICS	crotalus, sistrurus
HEADING/SUBHEADING	Chapter Two: Rattlesnakes/Rattlesnake Habitats, Keeping Predators Away
FOOTNOTE	Some rattlesnakes camouflage themselves to avoid predators.

Practice Questions

10.

INDEX

B	I	S
basic operation....7	installation 7	SIM card..................9
battery 7	Internet...................8	smartphone 7
C	**L**	**T**
call log 9	landline 5	text message 10
cell phone.............7	**M**	touch screen..........9
contacts................9	memory card........8	**V**
cordless phones ..6	**P**	voicemail...............10
D	pay phone 6	**W**
delete info 9	**R**	WiFi...........................8
dialing numbers ..9	receiver..................5	wireless network..8
H	ringtone 9	
handset 10	rotary phone..........5	

What inference can be made about this book based on its index?

A) The book is about different types of phones.

B) The book is about modern-day mobile phones.

C) The book is about the history of cell phones.

D) The book is about how to contact someone via phone.

11. Popular stories like *The Three Little Pigs* are often retold and changed into what are known as *twisted* fairy tales. *The Three Little Javelinas* is a tale similar to *The Three Little Pigs*, but it has a different setting and characters. It takes place in a desert instead of a forest, and the javelinas outsmart a coyote instead of a wolf.

    Italics are used in the text to indicate which of the following?

    A) titles and references to footnotes

    B) foreign phrases

    C) emphasized words and titles

    D) scientific terms

MEANING OF WORDS

To understand the meanings of unfamiliar words, use **CONTEXT CLUES**. Context clues are hints the author provides to help readers define difficult words. They can be found in words or phrases in the same sentence or in a neighboring sentence. Look for synonyms, antonyms, definitions, examples, and explanations in the text to determine the meaning of the unfamiliar word.

Sometimes parts of a word can make its meaning easier to determine. **AFFIXES** are added to **ROOT WORDS** (a word's basic form) to modify meaning. **PREFIXES** are added to the beginning of root words, while **SUFFIXES** are added to the ending. Divide words into parts, finding meaning in each part. Take, for example, the word *unjustifiable*: the prefix is *un–* (*not*), the root word is *justify* ("to prove reasonable"), and the suffix is *–able* ("referring to a quality").

> ⚠️
> Use what you know about a word to figure out its meaning, then look for clues in the sentence or paragraph.

Another way to determine the meaning of unknown words is to consider their denotation and connotation with other words in the sentence. **DENOTATION** is the literal meaning of a word, while **CONNOTATION** is the positive or negative associations of a word.

Authors use words to convey thoughts, but the meaning may be different from the literal meaning of the words. This is called **FIGURATIVE LANGUAGE**. Types of figurative language include similes, metaphors, hyperboles, and personification.

Similes compare two things that are not alike with the words *like* or *as*. Metaphors are used to compare two things that are not exactly alike but may share a certain characteristic.

Hyperboles are statements that exaggerate something in order to make a point or draw attention to a certain feature. Personification involves using human characteristics to describe an animal or object.

Table 1.6. Meanings of Words

Have you ever gone to a flea market? There are rows of furniture, clothing, and antiques waiting for discovery. Unlike a museum with items on display, flea markets are opportunities to learn and shop. Vendors bring their handmade goods to this communal event to show their crafts and make money.

CONTEXT CLUES	Vendors are people who sell things; people shop at a flea market.
AFFIXES	The prefix *com–* in *communal* means *with* or *together*.
MEANING	*Communal* means "shared with a community."

Practice Questions

12. The Bastille, Paris's famous historical prison, was originally built in 1370 as a fortification—called a *bastide* in Old French—to protect the city from English invasion. It rose 100 feet into the air, had eight towers, and was surrounded by a moat more than eighty feet wide. In the seventeenth century, the government **converted** the fortress into an elite prison for upper-class felons, political disruptors, and spies.

    Which word or phrase can be used to determine the meaning of *converted*?

    A) originally built

    B) fortification

    C) felons

    D) historical prison

13. Breaking a world record is no easy feat. An application and video submission of an amazing skill may not be enough. Potential record breakers may need to demonstrate their skill in front of an official world records judge. The judge will watch a performance of a record attempt to determine if the record-breaking claim is **credible**. After all evidence is collected, reviewed, and approved, a certificate for the new world record is granted!

    Based on affixes and context clues, what does *credible* mean?

    A) believable

    B) achievable

    C) likeable

    D) noticeable

14. Every year people gather in Durham Park to participate in the Food Truck Rodeo. A band plays, and the food trucks are like a carnival of delicious treats. The aroma of food draws all who pass by, creating a large crowd. The event is free to attend; patrons pay only for what they want to eat. From pizzas and burgers to hotdogs and pastries, there's something for everyone!

    Which type of figurative language is used in the second sentence?

    A) hyperbole

    B) metaphor

    C) personification

    D) simile

RECOGNIZING SEQUENCES

Look for **SIGNAL WORDS** that indicate steps of a process. These words will tell you when things need to happen in a certain order. Signal words should show a transition from one event or step to another.

⚠️

To find signal words, ask, *What happened first and what happened after that?*

When reading a passage, you will find that signal words can be used to follow the direction of the author's ideas and the sequence of events. Signal words show time order and how details flow in a chronological way.

Table 1.7. Following Directions and Recognizing Sequences

NASA wanted to launch a man from Earth to the moon. At first NASA used satellites for launch tests. Then in June of 1968, astronauts aboard the Apollo 8 launched into space and circled the moon ten times before returning to Earth. Finally, in 1969 three astronauts reached the moon in the Apollo 11 spacecraft. After a successful landing, two members of the crew walked on the moon. During their walk, they collected data and samples of rocks. They returned as heroes of space exploration.

signal words	*At first, Then, Finally, After, During*

Practice Questions

15.

> **FANTASTIC HARD-BOILED EGGS**
>
> **Ingredients**
>
> 6 eggs
>
> **Steps**
>
> Place the eggs at the bottom of a saucepan.
>
> Fill the saucepan with enough water to cover the eggs.
>
> Heat the saucepan on high heat until the water comes to a boil.
>
> After the water comes to a boil, turn the burner down to medium heat and continue boiling for 8 minutes.
>
> Strain the water from the pan, and run cold water over the eggs to cool them.
>
> Peel the eggs under a little running water.
>
> Serve.

According to the recipe, which action should be completed first?

A) Peel eggs under water.

B) Fill the saucepan with water.

C) Heat the water to a boil.

D) Strain the water from the pan.

16. Babies learn to move their bodies over time. Head control is first developed at two months to create strong neck, back, and tummy muscles. Next, the abilities to reach, grasp, and sit up with support happen around four to six months. By the end of six months, babies learn to roll over. After six to nine months, babies can sit on their own and crawl. During age nine to twelve months, pulling and standing up are mastered. Finally, after gaining good balance, babies take their first steps!

Which BEST describes the order of a baby's movement over time?

A) roll over, control head, sit up, crawl

B) sit up, roll over, crawl, walk

C) control head, reach, crawl, roll over

D) sit up, grasp, crawl, walk

Interpreting Verbal and Graphic Communications

Verbal communications can be used to send a message or information to an individual or a group. Memos, advertisements, and flyers are all ways in which ideas and information can be shared. Key elements include the heading, subject, date, message, pictures, and a call to action (information telling readers how to respond).

To better understand what is written, try to identify the author's intention and the purpose of the text. The structure of the text will help clarify the main points. Important parts may be presented in paragraphs, bullet points, or bold print.

Graphic communications are used to locate places, identify parts of an object, and demonstrate processes. Key parts include graphics, labels, numerical data, colors, symbols, and lines that show direction, connections, or relationships among parts.

Table 1.8. Interpreting Verbal and Graphic Communications

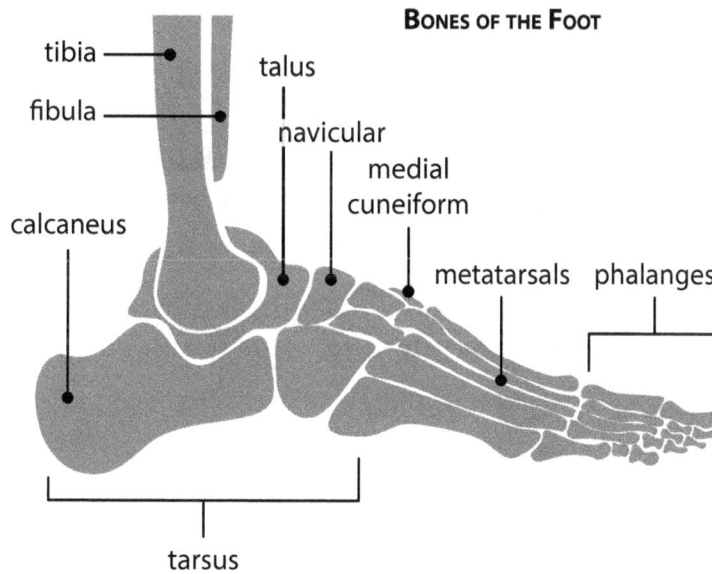

BONES OF THE FOOT

tibia

talus

fibula

navicular

medial cuneiform

calcaneus

metatarsals   phalanges

tarsus

HEADING	Bones of the Foot
PICTURE	visual representation of the parts of the foot
LINES/BRACKETS	outlining sections of the foot
LABELS	providing the name of each part of the foot

Practice Questions

17.

To: All Employees

From: Dennis Frazier, Manager

Date: 08/28/17

Re: Email Communication

This is a reminder of our Email Policy.

1. Please refrain from sending company-related emails through personal email accounts. Use company-assigned email accounts for all correspondence.
2. Please email managers and team leaders about time off at least three days in advance. Last-minute emails or phone calls are not acceptable.
3. Please respond to emails within forty-eight hours, as some are time-sensitive.

Thank you in advance for helping us all work better together!

Which best describes the writer's purpose?

A) to ensure that all employees use email properly

B) to persuade employees to use email more

C) to show appreciation for employees working together

D) to inform all employees of a new email policy

18.

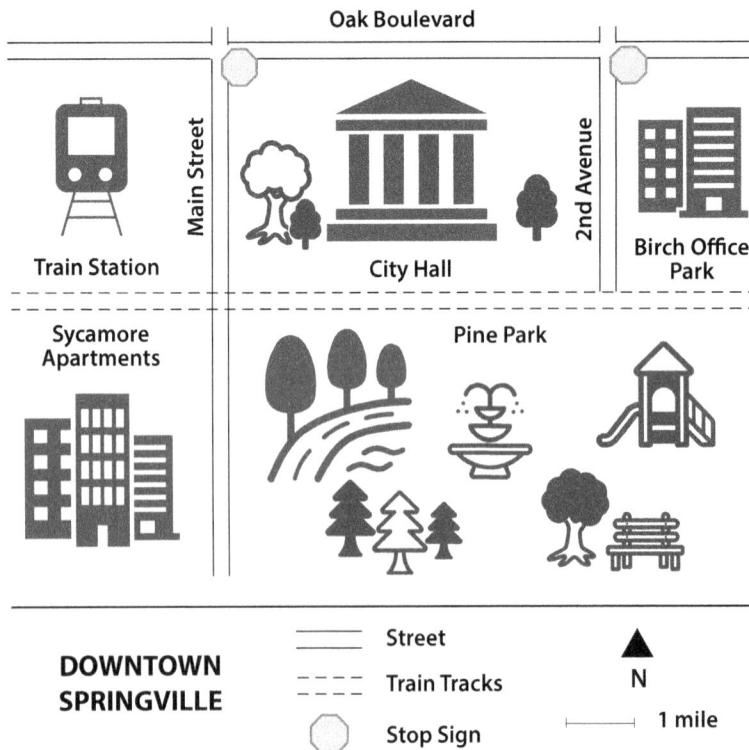

Jean works at the Birch Office Park and has to go to the train station to go home. If she walks on Oak Boulevard, how many stop signs will she pass?

A) 2

B) 3

C) 4

D) 5

ANSWER KEY

1. **B)** **Correct.** The topic of the passage is geysers. Tourists, volcanic eruptions, and super volcanos are all mentioned in the explanation of what geysers are and how they are formed.

2. **D)** **Correct.** The author writes that "the allied tribes...decisively defeated their US foes," and the remainder of the passage provides details to support this idea.

3. **C)** **Correct.** The passage specifically presents this detail as one of the advantages of subcontracting services.

4. **A)** **Correct.** The statement "It is a great way to advertise their food" is a judgment about how the shops use chalk to show menu items to customers. The word *great* expresses a feeling, and the idea cannot be proven.

5. **D)** **Correct.** After the war, there was a lack of focus on the world and greater focus on personal comforts, which writers viewed as superficiality and materialism.

6. **D)** **Correct.** The text provides details on the experiment as well as its results.

7. **C)** **Correct.** The author states that recycling and reusing objects reduce waste, which helps the environment.

8. **B)** **Correct.** The author demonstrates disapproval of film portrayals of gorillas and how they influence people's views of gorillas.

9. **D)** **Correct.** In this text, two brands of cream are being compared and contrasted.

10. **A)** **Correct.** While phone features are mentioned, the book is about the types of phones listed in the index.

11. **C)** **Correct.** Italics are used to highlight the titles of the books and to emphasize the word *twisted*, which refers to altering a story, not to something being misshapen.

12. **A)** **Correct.** *Fortification* and *fortress* are synonyms. In the seventeenth century, the purpose of the fortress changed. This is a clue that *converted* means "a change in form or function."

13. **A)** **Correct.** The root *cred* means *believe*. The words *evidence*, *reviewed*, and *approved* are context clues hinting that something needs to be believed and accepted.

14. **D)** **Correct.** The author compares the food trucks to "a carnival of delicious treats" using the word *like*.

15. **B)** **Correct.** According to the recipe directions, the saucepan must be filled with water before the other steps listed can occur.

16. **B) Correct.** According to the passage, a baby achieves milestones in independent movement in this order. Use the ages and signal words to determine the order of events.

17. **A) Correct.** The memo is intended to ensure that all employees are following the same email guidelines. It is a reminder of the existing policy, not a new policy, and includes instructions all employees must follow.

18. **A) Correct.** She will pass two stop signs; one at 2nd Avenue and one at Main Street.

LISTENING AND SPEAKING

INTRO TO TOEFL LISTENING SECTION

What's on the TOEFL Listening Section?

The listening section of the TOEFL will consist of thirty to forty questions and lasts forty to sixty minutes. Your test may include extra Listening questions that do not count toward your score. ETS uses these unscored questions to test new questions for future tests. However, you will not know which questions are unscored, so you must answer all the questions on this section. The questions on the listening portion of the test are multiple choice.

The test is divided into two or three sections: one conversation and one or two lectures. The conversation will most likely be related to education or training. The discussion might be about selecting classes for a degree program or how to handle a challenging assignment. The lecture or lectures are generally on an academic subject. Expect a lesson or lecture presented by a teacher, professor, or someone similar.

Vocabulary in all sections will often focus on wants, needs, preferences, and requirements, so associated terms should be expected on the exam and therefore practiced. Vocabulary associated with common academic settings (e.g., school registrar's office, tutoring center, and so forth) should be practiced and expected. Lectures and conversations will focus on events in the past, present, and future, so examinees should expect to hear many different verb tenses.

Examinees should also be prepared to hear multiple accents and voices. Speakers will include men, women, young people, older people, and both native and non-native English speakers with accents from various regions.

The test will assess not only an overall understanding of what is said but also an understanding of main ideas and the specific points made by speakers and their overall attitudes.

Each section will be played only one time, but specific questions may replay a portion of the lecture or conversation.

Tips for the TOEFL Listening Section

To prepare for the TOEFL listening portion, one should listen to as many conversations and lectures as possible. Additionally, test-takers should consider the various opportunities to hear English being spoken in similar contexts. Such situations include:

- television programs;
- online videos (e.g., YouTube);
- radio programs and podcasts;
- audio recordings of speeches or audio books; and
- audio- or video-recorded lectures or lessons by teachers or professors.

INTRO TO TOEFL SPEAKING SECTION

What's on the TOEFL Speaking Section?

On the speaking portion of the TOEFL, you will be asked four questions. The first question is about a familiar topic. The examiner will make introductions and ask general questions. These questions will typically focus on individual circumstances and interests. The examinee should be prepared to answer questions clearly, coherently, and using strong vocabulary about:

- family (e.g., spouse, siblings, parents)
- hobbies/interests (e.g., sports, activities)
- future plans (e.g., school, work)
- other familiar topics (e.g., the day's weather, the temperature of the room)

The second and third questions are based on a text and a related short conversation or lecture. Expect to read and hear about a change on campus or an academic topic. You will read the text and then listen to the accompanying conversation or lecture. You must then respond to a question about the information you have encountered. You will have fifteen to thirty seconds to prepare your response. You will not be able to refer to the information, but you can take notes while you are reading and listening. Expect to combine information from both the textual and audio source to answer the question correctly.

The fourth question asks you to respond to part of a lecture on an academic topic. You will have fifteen to thirty seconds to prepare your response after you listen to the lecture. Be prepared to summarize the main points of the material that you hear. Be ready to provide robust and well-considered responses.

Scoring on this portion of the exam is based on overall English-speaking skills as well as the ability to organize ideas, state opinions, and support those statements. The examinee's opinions themselves are NOT part of the score on the exam.

Vocabulary related to personal feelings and beliefs as well as basic transitional phrases (e.g., *also, additionally, furthermore,* and so forth) are important in the speaking section. Command of all verb tenses is also critical since discussions may focus on topics or beliefs about events or situations of the past, present, or future.

Tips for the TOEFL Speaking Section

Practicing for the speaking section of the exam requires examinees to do a lot of talking! Having frequent conversations in English is certainly helpful. In such conversations, it is a good idea to practice stating opinions or preferences and explaining the "why" behind them. It is also helpful to practice using a variety of verb tenses and switching between these tenses as the conversation requires.

To practice, examinees do not need a partner. They do, however, need to practice speaking about a variety of topics and can use video or audio to record themselves or even practice in front of a mirror. Some suggestions for speaking practice include:

- past positive experiences (e.g., helping others, when others have helped you);
- large projects or events with which you have been involved;
- teams or groups of which you have been a member;
- things you have learned (e.g., skills, hobbies, teamwork);
- challenges you have overcome;
- people you know;
- customs/celebrations/food from your country of origin; and
- things you like/dislike about technology.

When practicing, you must be sure to time each speech and aim to speak for two minutes.

Keep in mind that the examiner will evaluate speakers on language skills, not opinions. Don't worry about trying to "please" or "agree with" the examiner—this will cause unnecessary anxiety! Focus on preparing to speak on a wide variety of topics, even those which are unfamiliar.

It is also wise to practice using FILLERS, or HESITATION DEVICES. These are words or phrases that effectively create brief moments of time for thinking about what to say next. Some common examples are:

- That's a good question.
- Let me think about that.
- That's an interesting question.
- I'll have to think about that for a minute.
- Well...
- You see...
- So, basically...

WRITING

On the Writing section, the TOEFL asks you to complete two tasks. The first task tests your ability to **WRITE BASED ON READING AND LISTENING** to outside sources. You must review written and spoken material—a text and a lecture. You will answer a question based on the text and lecture. Be ready to summarize main points and important information. The second writing task is an **INDEPENDENT WRITING TASK**. You must write an essay expressing your opinion or perspective on an issue. You will be provided with a prompt and asked to take a position on it. You may use your own experiences, knowledge, and opinions to craft your response.

THE WRITING TASKS

On the exam, you will encounter a text and a recorded lecture about an academic topic. This is the Writing Based on Reading and Listening task. You must summarize what you read and hear in approximately 150 – 225 words. To accomplish this task, use descriptive language, clarity, and structure. Focus on accuracy, clarity, and emphasizing the main points. Be sure to take into account information from both the text and the lecture. Imagine you are explaining the topic to a person who has not read the text or heard the lecture.

On the other hand, to do well on the independent writing task, you must take a clear side on the issue put forth in the prompt. Support your perspective with strong arguments and specific examples. An effective response is clearly organized and structured, displays strong vocabulary, and features complex sentences. It should be about 300 words long.

> ⚠ There are two common types of essays. An **expository** essay explains an issue without taking sides or promoting a perspective. A **persuasive** essay argues in favor of or against an issue or perspective. For the TOEFL, you'll be writing a persuasive essay.

WRITING AN ESSAY

A **THESIS STATEMENT** articulates the main argument of the essay. No essay is complete without it: the structure and organization of the essay revolve around the thesis statement.

The thesis statement is simply the writer's main idea or argument. It usually appears at the end of the introduction.

In a good thesis statement, the author states his or her idea or argument and why it is correct or true.

Example

Take a position on the following topic in your essay. You can choose to write about either of the two viewpoints discussed in the prompt, or you may argue for a third point of view.

Many scientists argue that recent unusual weather patterns, such as powerful hurricanes and droughts, are due to climate change triggered by human activity. They argue that automobiles, oil and gas production, and manufacturing generate carbon emissions that artificially heat the atmosphere, resulting in extreme weather patterns. Others disagree. Some researchers and media pundits argue that climate change is natural, and that extreme weather has always been a feature of Earth's atmosphere.

Possible thesis statements:

- Around the world more people than ever before are driving cars, and industrial production is at an all-time high; it is obvious that human activity is affecting the atmosphere and causing extreme weather events.

- I believe that temperatures and storms are more extreme than ever because of the environmental impact of human activity; not only do scientists have overwhelming evidence that climate change is unnatural, but I can also personally remember when there were fewer storms and variations in temperature.

- Society needs cars and manufacturing, but governments should restrict harmful emissions released into the atmosphere so we can slow down climate change and save lives.

STRUCTURING THE ESSAY

On the TOEFL, a strong essay will have an introduction, a body, and a conclusion. While there are many ways to organize an essay, on this exam it is most important that the essay is clearly structured. There is no need to get too complicated: the following simple structure will do.

Introduction

Some writers struggle with the introduction, but it is the best opportunity to present your idea or argument. For the TOEFL essay, the introduction can be one paragraph that ends with the thesis statement. In the body of the paragraph, the writer should provide some context for his or her argument. This context might include counterarguments, a preview of specific examples to be discussed later on, acknowledgement of the complexities of the issue, or even a reference to personal experience. The writer can reexamine some of these issues in the conclusion.

> ⚠ If you're not sure what to include in your introduction, start your essay with just the thesis statement. You can go back and complete the introduction once the rest of the essay is finished.

Example

In the example below, the writer has written an introduction that includes context for her argument: background information, a counterargument, and personal experience. As a result, the reader has a better idea of how complex the issue is and why the writer feels the way she does. The thesis statement appears at the end of the paragraph and, thanks to the introduction as a whole, has more impact.

A century ago, there were barely any cars on the road. Oil had just been discovered in a few parts of the world. Industrial production existed but had not yet exploded with the introduction of the assembly line. Refineries and factories were not yet churning out the chemical emissions they are today. Certainly, hurricanes and droughts occurred, but the populations and infrastructure affected were far smaller. Now, scientists have evidence that human activity—like pollution from industry and cars—is affecting the atmosphere and making weather more extreme. In 2017, millions of people were affected by hurricanes and wildfires. It is true that some researchers disagree that human activity has caused these and other extreme weather events. But why take the risk? If we can limit destruction now and in the future, we should. Extreme weather events are a danger to people all around the world. Society needs cars and manufacturing, but governments should restrict harmful emissions released into the atmosphere so we can slow down climate change and save lives.

The Body Paragraphs

Most writers find the body of the essay the easiest part to write. The body of the essay is simply several paragraphs, each beginning with a topic sentence to address an example that supports the argument made in the thesis statement or, in the case of an expository essay, explains the writer's reasoning. On the TOEFL, you may use specific examples, personal anecdotes, present problems and solutions, or compare and contrast ideas. You do not need to refer to any outside literature or documentation.

To strengthen the body of the essay, writers should maintain consistency in paragraphs by always beginning with a topic sentence to introduce the main idea of each paragraph. Each paragraph deals with its own main topic, but writers should use transition words and phrases to link paragraphs with each other. A good essay maintains readability and flow.

Example

This example body paragraph is related to the introduction provided above. It provides reasoning and historical evidence for the author's argument that human activity is negatively impacting the earth and causing climate change.

Human industrial activity has been growing exponentially, putting more pollution into the atmosphere than ever. Over the past forty years, large countries like China and India have become industrialized and manufacture many of the world's products. As their populations become more prosperous, demand for automobiles also rises, putting more cars on the road—and exhaust in the air. While industrial development has benefitted Asia and other areas, carbon emissions that cause climate change have multiplied. Meanwhile, previously industrialized countries in Europe and North America continue to produce carbon emissions. In the nineteenth century, only a few countries had industrial sectors; today, global industry strains the environment like never before. The past 150 years have seen unprecedented industrial growth. Even if the climate changes naturally over time, it cannot be denied that recent human activity has suddenly generated enormous amounts of carbon emissions that have impacted the atmosphere. Scientists say that the earth is warming as a result.

Conclusion

The conclusion does not need to be long. Its purpose is to wrap up the essay, reminding the reader why the topic and the writer's discussion are important. It is an opportunity for the writer to reexamine the thesis statement and ideas posited in the introduction. It is a time to reinforce the argument, not just to repeat the introduction.

Example

This example is taken from the same essay as the introduction and body paragraph above. It reinforces the writer's argument without simply repeating what she said in the introduction. The writer does address the topics she spoke about in the introduction (climate change and protecting people from extreme weather) but she does not simply rewrite the thesis; rather, she calls for action.

No doubt, scientists, pundits, and politicians will continue to argue over the reasons for extreme weather. Meanwhile, Mother Nature will continue to wreak havoc on vulnerable areas regardless of what we think. Because we have proof that climate change is related to extreme weather and we know that extreme weather threatens people's lives, the time to act is now. We can take steps to mitigate pollution without lowering quality of life. Doing anything else is irresponsible—and for some, deadly.

PROVIDING SUPPORTING EVIDENCE

As discussed above, a good essay should have specific evidence or examples that support the thesis statement. On the TOEFL, a specific example should be something related to the idea of the paragraph and the essay, not a new idea. A specific example can be from your general knowledge; you do not need to know about specific academic issues to do well on the essay. Remember, you are being tested on your language and reasoning skills.

The following are some examples of general statements and specific statements that provide more detailed support:

GENERAL: Human industrial activity has been growing exponentially, putting more pollution into the atmosphere than ever.

SPECIFIC: Over the past forty years, large countries like China and India have become industrialized and manufacture many of the world's products. As their populations become more prosperous, demand for automobiles also rises, putting more cars on the road—and exhaust in the air.

SPECIFIC: Meanwhile, previously industrialized countries in Europe and North America continue to produce carbon emissions. In the nineteenth century, only a few countries had industrial sectors; today, global industry strains the environment like never before.

GENERAL: More people than ever are affected by extreme weather.

SPECIFIC: In 2017, several hurricanes affected the United States and the Caribbean. In Texas, Hurricane Harvey led to historic flooding in Houston and the Texas Coast. Millions of people were affected; thousands lost their homes, jobs, and livelihoods.

SPECIFIC: Hurricane Irma damaged the US Virgin Islands and neighboring Caribbean nations. Soon after, Hurricane Maria catastrophically devastated Puerto Rico. Months later, Puerto Ricans were still without power and basic necessities. It is still not clear how many have died due to the storm and related damage.

Example

The paragraph below is structured with a topic sentence and specific supporting ideas. This paragraph supports the introduction in the example above.

More people than ever are affected by extreme weather. In 2017, several hurricanes affected the United States and the Caribbean. In Texas, Hurricane Harvey led to historic flooding in Houston and the Texas Coast. Millions of people were affected; thousands lost their homes, jobs, and livelihoods. Hurricane Irma damaged Florida, the US Virgin Islands and neighboring Caribbean nations. Soon after, Hurricane Maria catastrophically devastated Puerto Rico. Months later, Puerto Ricans were still without power and basic necessities. It is still not clear how many have died due to the storm and related damage. In California, severe droughts led to exceptionally large wildfires that threatened Los Angeles and destroyed neighboring communities. Meanwhile, those same areas—Southern California, the Texas Coast, and Florida—continue to grow, putting more people at risk when the next hurricane or fire strikes.

WRITING WELL

Using transitions, complex sentences, and certain words can turn a good description or essay into a great one. Transitions, syntax, word choice, and tone all help clarify and amplify a writer's argument or point and improve the flow of any piece of writing.

Transitions

An essay consists of several paragraphs. **TRANSITIONS** are words and phrases that help connect the paragraphs and ideas of the text. Most commonly, transitions appear at the beginning of a paragraph, but writers should also use them throughout a text to connect overarching ideas. Common transition words include *also, next, still, although, in addition to*, and *in other words*. A transition shows a relationship between ideas, so writers should pay close attention to the transition words and phrases they choose. Transitions may show connections or contrasts between words and ideas.

Table 3.1. Common Transitions

TRANSITION TYPE	EXAMPLES
addition	additionally, also, as well, further, furthermore, in addition, moreover
cause and effect	as a result, because, consequently, due to, if/then, so, therefore, thus
concluding	briefly, finally, in conclusion, in summary, thus, to conclude
contrast	but, however, in contrast, nevertheless, on the contrary, on the other hand, yet
examples	for example, for instance, in other words
similarity	also, likewise, similarly
time	after, before, currently, later, recently, since, subsequently, then, while

Syntax

SYNTAX refers to how words and phrases are arranged in writing or speech. Writing varied sentences is essential to capturing and keeping a reader's interest. A good essay features different types of sentences: simple, complex, compound, and compound-complex. Sentences need not always begin with the subject; they might start with a transition word or phrase, for instance. Variety is key.

Still, writers should keep in mind that the point of an essay is to convey an idea to the reader, so it is most important that the writing be clear. Clarity should not be sacrificed for the sake of flowery, overly wordy language or confusing syntax.

Word Choice and Tone

Like syntax, WORD CHOICE makes an impression on readers. The TOEFL does not test on specific vocabulary or require writers to use specific words on the essay. However, the essay is a good opportunity to use strong vocabulary related to the prompt or issue under discussion. Writers should be careful, though, and have confidence that they understand the words they are using. Writers should also avoid vague, imprecise, or generalizing language like *good*, *bad*, *a lot*, *a little*, *very*, *normal*, and so on.

Editing, Revising, and Proofreading

On the TOEFL, the writer has twenty minutes to complete the Writing Based on Reading and Listening task and thirty minutes to complete the Independent Writing task. If there is time for editing or proofreading, writers should hunt for grammar, spelling, or punctuation mistakes that could change the meaning of the text or make it difficult to understand. These include errors such as sentence fragments, run-on sentences, subject-verb disagreement, and pronoun-antecedent disagreement.

4

PRACTICE TEST ONE

READING

DIRECTIONS: Read the passage and/or figure, and then answer the question.

Snakes

Skin coloration and markings have an important role to play in the world of snakes. Those intricate diamonds, stripes, and swirls help the animals hide from predators, but perhaps most importantly (for us humans, anyway), the markings can also indicate whether the snake is venomous. While it might seem counterintuitive for a venomous snake to stand out in bright red or blue, that fancy costume tells any nearby predator that approaching him would be a bad idea.

If you see a flashy-looking snake in the woods, though, those markings don't necessarily mean it's venomous: some snakes have found a way to ward off predators without the actual venom. The scarlet kingsnake, for example, has very similar markings to the venomous coral snake with whom it frequently shares a habitat. However, the kingsnake is actually nonvenomous; it's merely pretending to be dangerous to eat. A predatory hawk or eagle, usually hunting from high in the sky, can't tell the difference between the two species, and so the kingsnake gets passed over and lives another day.

1. What is the author's primary purpose in writing this essay?

   A) to explain how the markings on a snake are related to whether it's venomous

   B) to teach readers the difference between coral snakes and kingsnakes

   C) to illustrate why snakes are dangerous

   D) to demonstrate how animals survive in difficult environments

2. What can the reader conclude from the passage above?

   A) The kingsnake is dangerous to humans.

   B) The coral snake and the kingsnake are both hunted by the same predators.

   C) It's safe to handle snakes in the woods because you can easily tell whether they're poisonous.

   D) The kingsnake changes its markings when hawks or eagles are close by.

3. What is the best summary of this passage?

   A) Humans can use coloration and markings on snakes to determine whether they're venomous.

   B) Animals often use coloration to hide from predators.

   C) The scarlet kingsnake and the coral snake have nearly identical markings.

   D) Venomous snakes often have bright markings, although nonvenomous snakes can also mimic those colors.

4. Which statement is NOT a detail from the passage?

   A) Predators will avoid eating kingsnakes because their markings are like those on coral snakes.

   B) Kingsnakes and coral snakes live in the same habitats.

   C) The coral snake uses its coloration to hide from predators.

   D) The kingsnake is not venomous.

5. What is the meaning of the word *intricate* in the first paragraph?

   A) complex

   B) colorful

   C) purposeful

   D) changeable

6. What is the difference between kingsnakes and coral snakes according to the passage?

   A) Both kingsnakes and coral snakes are nonvenomous, but coral snakes have colorful markings.

   B) Both kingsnakes and coral snakes are venomous, but kingsnakes have colorful markings.

   C) Kingsnakes are nonvenomous while coral snakes are venomous.

   D) Coral snakes are nonvenomous while kingsnakes are venomous.

Taking Temperature

Taking a person's temperature is one of the most basic and common health care tasks. Everyone from nurses to emergency medical technicians to concerned parents should be able to grab a thermometer to take a patient or loved one's temperature. But what's the best way to get an accurate reading? The answer depends on the situation.

The most common way people measure body temperature is orally. A simple digital or disposable thermometer is placed under the tongue for a few minutes, and the task is done. There are many situations, however, when measuring temperature orally isn't an option. For example, when a person can't breathe through his nose, he won't be able to keep his mouth closed long enough to get an accurate reading. In these situations, it's often preferable to place the thermometer in the rectum or armpit. Using the rectum also has the added benefit of providing a much more accurate reading than other locations can provide.

It's also often the case that certain people, like agitated patients or fussy babies, won't be able to sit still long enough for an accurate reading. In these situations, it's best to use a thermometer that works much more quickly, such as one that measures temperature in the ear or at the temporal artery. No matter which method is chosen, however, it's important to check the average temperature for each region, as it can vary by several degrees.

7. Match the site on the body for taking temperature to the phrase that best characterizes it.

most accurate site for taking temperature	
most common site for taking temperature	
acceptable site for taking temperature	

   ▪ temporal artery

   ▪ mouth

   ▪ rectum

8. Which statement is a detail from the passage? Choose THREE answers.

A) Taking a temperature in the ear or at the temporal artery is more accurate than taking it orally.

B) The most common way to measure temperature is by placing a thermometer in the mouth.

C) If an individual cannot breathe through the nose, taking his or her temperature orally will likely give an inaccurate reading.

D) The standard human body temperature varies depending on whether it's measured in the mouth, rectum, armpit, ear, or temporal artery.

E) Failing to account for a patient's weight or height can cause a false reading.

9. What is the author's primary purpose in writing this essay?

A) to advocate for the use of thermometers that measure temperature in the ear or at the temporal artery

B) to explain the methods available to measure a person's temperature and the situation where each method is appropriate

C) to warn readers that the average temperature of the human body varies by region

D) to discuss how nurses use different types of thermometers depending on the type of patient they are examining

10. What is the best summary of this passage?

A) It's important that everyone know the best way to take a person's temperature in any given situation.

B) The most common method of taking a person's temperature—orally—isn't appropriate in some situations.

C) The most accurate way to take a temperature is placing a digital thermometer in the rectum.

D) There are many different ways to take a person's temperature, and which is appropriate will depend on the situation.

11. What is the meaning of the word *agitated* in the last paragraph?

A) obviously upset

B) quickly moving

C) violently ill

D) slightly dirty

12. According to the passage, why is it sometimes preferable to take a person's temperature rectally?

A) Rectal readings are more accurate than oral readings.

B) Many people cannot sit still long enough to have their temperatures taken orally.

C) Temperature readings can vary widely between regions of the body.

D) Many people do not have access to quick-acting thermometers.

Water and the Solar System

The following passage and table are adapted from an article entitled "The Solar System and Beyond Is Awash with Water," published by NASA in April 2015.

As NASA missions explore our solar system and search for new worlds, they are finding water in surprising places. Water is but one piece of our search for habitable planets and life beyond Earth, yet it links many seemingly unrelated worlds in surprising ways.

"NASA science activities have provided a wave of amazing findings related to water in recent years that inspire us to continue investigating our origins and the fascinating possibilities for other worlds, and life, in the universe," said Ellen Stofan, chief scientist for the agency. "In our lifetime, we may very well finally answer whether we are alone in the solar system and beyond."

The chemical elements in water, hydrogen and oxygen, are some of the most abundant elements in the universe. Astronomers see the signature of water in giant molecular clouds between the stars, in disks of material that represent newborn planetary systems, and in the atmospheres of giant planets orbiting other stars.

There are several worlds thought to possess liquid water beneath their surfaces, and many more that have water in the form of ice or vapor. Water is found in primitive bodies like comets and asteroids, and dwarf planets like Ceres. The atmospheres and interiors of the four giant planets—Jupiter, Saturn, Uranus and Neptune—are thought to contain enormous quantities of the wet stuff, and their moons and rings have substantial water ice.

Perhaps the most surprising water worlds are the five icy moons of Jupiter and Saturn that show strong evidence of oceans beneath their surfaces: Ganymede, Europa and Callisto at Jupiter, and Enceladus and Titan at Saturn.

Scientists using NASA's Hubble Space Telescope recently provided powerful evidence that Ganymede has a saltwater, sub-surface ocean, likely sandwiched between two layers of ice.

Europa and Enceladus are thought to have an ocean of liquid water beneath their surface in contact with mineral-rich rock, and may have the three ingredients needed for life as we know it: liquid water, essential chemical elements for biological processes, and sources of energy that could be used by living things.

Understanding the distribution of water in our solar system tells us a great deal about how the planets, moons, comets and other bodies formed 4.5 billion years ago from the disk of gas and dust that surrounded our sun. The space closer to the sun was hotter and drier than the space farther from the sun, which was cold enough for water to condense. The dividing line, called the "frost line," sat around Jupiter's present-day orbit. Even today, this is the approximate distance from the sun at which the ice on most comets begins to melt and become "active." Their brilliant spray releases water ice, vapor, dust and other chemicals, which are thought to form the bedrock of most worlds of the frigid outer solar system.

Scientists think it was too hot in the solar system's early days for water to condense into liquid or ice on the inner planets, so it had to be delivered—possibly by comets and water-bearing asteroids. NASA's Dawn mission is currently studying Ceres, which is the largest body in the asteroid belt between Mars and Jupiter. Researchers think Ceres might have a water-rich composition similar to some of the bodies that brought water to the three rocky, inner planets, including Earth.

The amount of water in the giant planet Jupiter holds a critical missing piece to the puzzle of our solar system's formation. Jupiter was likely the first planet to form, and it contains most of the material that wasn't incorporated into the sun. The leading theories about its formation rest on the amount of water the planet soaked up.

It's easy to forget that the story of Earth's water, from gentle rains to raging rivers, is intimately connected to the larger story of our solar system and beyond. But our water came from somewhere—every world in our solar system got its water from the same shared source. So it's worth considering that the next glass of water you drink could easily have been part of a comet, or an ocean moon, or a long-vanished sea on the surface of Mars. And note that the night sky may be full of exoplanets formed by similar processes to our home world, where gentle waves wash against the shores of alien seas.

Moons of Jupiter and Saturn

NAME (DESCRIPTION)	DISTANCE FROM SUN (IN ASTRONOMICAL UNITS)	OCEAN WORLD STATUS
Europa (moon of Jupiter)	5.2 AU	Active
Ganymede (moon of Jupiter)	5.2 AU	Locked (under ice)
Callisto (moon of Jupiter)	5.2 AU	Locked (under ice)
Enceladus (moon of Saturn)	9.5 AU	Active
Titan (moon of Saturn)	9.5 AU	Locked (under ice)

13. Why does the author provide details in the third paragraph?

    A) to make the reader curious about celestial bodies and events

    B) to argue that the elements found in water are not plentiful within our solar system

    C) to remind the reader of the relative size of Earth in comparison to the rest of our solar system

    D) to illustrate the widespread availability of hydrogen and oxygen in space

14. What does the passage indicate about water?

    A) It can be found across our solar system in various forms.

    B) It is the most precious resource within our solar system.

    C) It is only available on our planet and the planets nearest to us.

    D) It is not a renewable resource.

15. Which excerpt from the text provides the best evidence for the answer to the previous question?

    A) "The chemical elements in water, hydrogen and oxygen, are some of the most abundant elements in the universe."

    B) "There are several worlds thought to possess liquid water beneath their surfaces, and many more that have water in the form of ice or vapor."

    C) "Scientists think it was too hot in the solar system's early days for water to condense into liquid or ice on the inner planets, so it had to be delivered—possibly by comets and water-bearing asteroids."

    D) "So it's worth considering that the next glass of water you drink could easily have been part of a comet, or an ocean moon, or a long-vanished sea on the surface of Mars."

16. According to the passage, what does water distribution in our solar system provide?

    A) an efficient system for recycling the precious resource

    B) an important clue about the formation of celestial bodies

    C) proof that life cannot survive outside the "frost line"

    D) plentiful opportunities for transporting the substance across great distances

17. The author indicates that, in addition to liquid water, terrestrial forms of life also require what in order to survive?

    A) certain chemical elements and useable energy sources

    B) substantial amounts of hydrogen and oxygen

    C) at least some sunlight

    D) frozen water

18. The author indicates that the frost line is

    A) a dividing line outside of which planets cannot sustain life.

    B) the only location in our solar system where liquid water and frozen water can exist simultaneously.

    C) the location at which most new bodies in our solar system form.

    D) the distance from the sun at which liquid water begins to freeze.

19. What does the passage indicate about Earth's liquid water?

    A) It was probably recycled from other planets.

    B) It may have been transported here by traveling, water-rich bodies like comets.

    C) It might have been found on Jupiter before it was carried across the solar system by comets.

    D) It could have been in the form of vapor until it reached our atmosphere.

20. What is the meaning of the word *bedrock* in paragraph 8?

A) pedestal

B) heart

C) anchor

D) foundation

21. Which conclusion is supported by both the passage and the table?

A) Celestial bodies that exist outside of the frost line are not likely to contain water in any form.

B) Jupiter's distance from the sun prevents it from hosting liquid water.

C) Evidence of water in some form has been found on a number of celestial bodies as far from the sun as Saturn.

D) Water is a rare and valuable substance in our solar system.

22. Which excerpt from the text provides the best evidence for the answer to the previous question?

A) "There are several worlds thought to possess liquid water beneath their surfaces, and many more that have water in the form of ice or vapor."

B) "Europa and Enceladus are thought to have…the three ingredients needed for life as we know it: liquid water, essential chemical elements for biological processes, and sources of energy that could be used by living things."

C) "Their brilliant spray releases water ice, vapor, dust and other chemicals, which are thought to form the bedrock of most worlds of the frigid outer solar system."

D) "Scientists think it was too hot in the solar system's early days for water to condense into liquid or ice on the inner planets, so it had to be delivered—possibly by comets and water-bearing asteroids."

Jazz

In recent decades, jazz has been associated with New Orleans and festivals like Mardi Gras, but in the 1920s, jazz was a booming trend whose influence reached into many aspects of American culture. In fact, the years between World War I and the Great Depression were known as the Jazz Age, a term coined by F. Scott Fitzgerald in his famous novel *The Great Gatsby*. Sometimes also called the Roaring Twenties, this time period saw major urban centers experiencing new economic, cultural, and artistic vitality. In the United States, musicians flocked to cities like New York and Chicago, which would become famous hubs for jazz musicians. Ella Fitzgerald, for example, moved from Virginia to New York City to begin her much-lauded singing career, and jazz pioneer Louis Armstrong got his big break in Chicago.

Jazz music was played by and for a more expressive and freed populace than the United States had previously seen. Women gained the right to vote and were openly seen drinking and dancing to jazz music. This period marked the emergence of the flapper, a woman determined to make a statement about her new role in society. Jazz music also provided the soundtrack for the explosion of African American art and culture now known as the Harlem Renaissance. In addition to Fitzgerald and Armstrong, numerous musicians, including Duke Ellington, Fats Waller, and Bessie Smith, promoted their distinctive and complex music as an integral part of the emerging African American culture.

23. Place the name of the public figure in the appropriate column. You may or may not fill up each column.

- Ella Fitzgerald
- F. Scott Fitzgerald
- Duke Ellington
- Bessie Smith
- Louis Armstrong

MUSICIANS	WRITERS

24. What is the main idea of the passage?

    A) People should associate jazz music with the 1920s, not modern New Orleans.

    B) Jazz music played an important role in many cultural movements of the 1920s.

    C) Many famous jazz musicians began their careers in New York City and Chicago.

    D) African Americans were instrumental in launching jazz into mainstream culture.

25. What is a reasonable inference that can be drawn from this passage?

    A) Jazz music was important to minority groups struggling for social equality in the 1920s.

    B) Duke Ellington, Fats Waller, and Bessie Smith were the most important jazz musicians of the Harlem Renaissance.

    C) Women gained the right to vote with the help of jazz musicians.

    D) Duke Ellington, Fats Waller, and Bessie Smith all supported women's right to vote.

26. What is the author's primary purpose in writing this essay?

    A) to explain the role jazz musicians played in the Harlem Renaissance

    B) to inform the reader about the many important musicians playing jazz in the 1920s

    C) to discuss how jazz influenced important cultural movements in the 1920s

    D) to provide a history of jazz music in the 20th century

27. Which of the following is NOT a fact stated in the passage?

    A) The years between World War I and the Great Depression were known as the Jazz Age.

    B) Ella Fitzgerald and Louis Armstrong both moved to New York City to start their music careers.

    C) Women danced to jazz music during the 1920s to make a statement about their role in society.

    D) Jazz music was an integral part of the emerging African American culture of the 1920s.

28. What can the reader conclude from the passage above?

    A) F. Scott Fitzgerald supported jazz musicians in New York and Chicago.

    B) Jazz music is no longer as popular as it once was.

    C) Both women and African Americans used jazz music as a way of expressing their newfound freedom.

    D) Flappers and African American musicians worked together to produce jazz music.

Arctic Marine Mammals

The following passage is adapted from an article entitled "NASA Contributes to First Global Review of Arctic Marine Mammals," published by NASA in April 2015.

Many human communities want answers about the current status and future of Arctic marine mammals, including scientists who dedicate their lives to studying them and indigenous people whose traditional ways of subsistence are intertwined with the fate of species such as ice seals, narwhals, walruses, and polar bears.

But there are many unknowns about the current status of eleven species of marine mammals who depend on Arctic sea ice to live, feed and breed, and about how their fragile habitat will evolve in a warming world.

A recently published multinational study attempted to gauge the population trends of Arctic marine mammals and changes in their habitat, identify missing scientific information, and provide recommendations for the conservation of Arctic marine mammals over the next decades.

The Arctic sea ice cover, made of frozen seawater floating on top of the Arctic Ocean and its neighboring seas, naturally grows in the fall and winter and melts during the spring and summer every year. But over the past decades, the melt season has grown longer and the average extent of Arctic sea ice has diminished, changing the game for many Arctic marine mammals—namely beluga, narwhal and bowhead whales; ringed, bearded, spotted, ribbon, harp and hooded seals; walruses; and polar bears.

"This research would not have been possible without support from NASA," said Kristin Laidre, lead author of the new study and a polar scientist with University of Washington in Seattle. "NASA backed us on research related to the biodiversity and ecology of Arctic marine mammals, as well as the development of metrics for the loss of sea ice, their habitat."

Laidre's team used the Arctic sea ice record derived from microwave measurements taken by NASA and Department of Defense satellites. This record began in late 1978, is uninterrupted, and relies on NASA-developed methods for processing the microwave data.

"It's really our best global view of the Arctic sea ice," said Harry Stern, author of the paper with Laidre and a mathematician specializing in sea ice and climate at University of Washington.

Stern divided the Arctic Ocean into twelve regions. Using daily sea ice concentration data from the satellite record, he calculated changes in the dates of the beginning of the melt season in spring and the start of the fall freeze-up from 1979 to 2013. He found that, in all regions but one, the melt season had grown longer (mostly by five to ten weeks, and by twenty weeks in one region).

"Sea ice is critical for Arctic marine mammals because events such as feeding, giving birth, molting, and resting are closely timed with the availability of their ice platform," Laidre said. "It is especially critical for the ice-dependent species—seals and polar bears. Ice seals use the sea ice platform to give birth and nurse pups during very specific weeks of the spring, and polar bears use sea ice for feeding, starting in late winter and continuing until the ice breaks up."

Pacific walrus use the floating pack ice both as a platform on which to rest between feeding bouts and as a passive transport around their habitat.

"Loss of sea ice has resulted in walrus hauling out on land in Alaska and Russia in massive numbers—these land haul outs result in trampling of their young," Laidre said. "Also, now walrus must travel a longer way to reach their feeding areas, which is energetically costly."

In the case of Arctic whales, the changes in sea ice might benefit their populations, at least in the short term: the loss and earlier retreat of sea ice opens up new habitats and, in some areas of the Arctic, has also led to an increase in food production and the length of their feeding season.

In the future, Stern said higher-resolution satellite microwave data might come in handy when studying the interactions of Arctic marine mammals with their icy habitat.

"For example, we know that narwhals congregate in specific areas of the Arctic in the wintertime, so maybe a higher spatial resolution in these areas might help us better understand their relationship with the ice," Stern said. "But mainly, just continuing daily coverage is what's important for the long-term monitoring of habitat changes."

29. Why does the author most likely include the list of Arctic marine mammals in paragraph 4?

   A) to illustrate a discrepancy between the number of Arctic species and the number of species that depend on sea ice for survival

   B) to challenge the assertion that the recession of sea ice is significant

   C) to articulate a general truth about life in the Arctic

   D) to highlight the number of species that depend on sea ice for their survival

30. Why does the author include a detail about indigenous people of the Arctic in the first paragraph?

A) to provide readers with a relatable story to consider as they read the article

B) to emphasize the importance of protecting the habitats of Arctic marine mammals

C) to challenge readers to make Arctic preservation efforts their top priority

D) to illustrate a contrast between the indigenous people and the scientists mentioned in the first part of the sentence

31. What does the passage indicate about research on sea ice and the animals that rely on sea ice?

A) Scientists know everything they need to know.

B) Data collection is rarely a simple process.

C) Very few answers currently exist.

D) Vigilant observation is an essential tool in gaining insight.

32. Which excerpt from the text provides the best evidence for the answer to the previous question?

A) "Using daily sea ice concentration data from the satellite record, he calculated changes in the dates of the beginning of the melt season in spring and the start of the fall freeze-up from 1979 to 2013."

B) "Sea ice is critical for Arctic marine mammals because events such as feeding, giving birth, molting, and resting are closely timed with the availability of their ice platform."

C) "The Arctic sea ice cover, made of frozen seawater floating on top of the Arctic Ocean and its neighboring seas, naturally grows in the fall and winter and melts during the spring and summer every year."

D) "But over the past decades, the melt season has grown longer and the average extent of Arctic sea ice has diminished, changing the game for many Arctic marine mammals."

33. What is the meaning of the word *fragile* in paragraph 2?

A) brittle

B) flimsy

C) breakable

D) unstable

34. The passage indicates that in a little over three decades, the length of the melt seasons in most regions of the Arctic

A) decreased by more than two months.

B) increased by more than two months.

C) decreased by more than a month.

D) increased by more than a month.

35. What is the meaning of the word *retreat* in paragraph 12?

A) surrender

B) refuge

C) recession

D) departure

36. Which excerpt from the text provides the best evidence for the answer to the previous question?

A) "But there are many unknowns about the current status of eleven species of marine mammals who depend on Arctic sea ice to live, feed and breed, and about how their fragile habitat will evolve in a warming world."

B) "Using daily sea ice concentration data from the satellite record, he calculated changes in the dates of the beginning of the melt season in spring and the start of the fall freeze-up from 1979 to 2013."

C) "In the future, Stern said higher-resolution satellite microwave data might come in handy when studying the interactions of Arctic marine mammals with their icy habitat."

D) "But mainly, just continuing daily coverage is what's important for the long-term monitoring of habitat changes."

37. What does the author indicate in paragraph 12?

    A) most, but not all, animals struggle when the availability of sea ice decreases.

    B) many animals will continue to thrive despite the change in climate.

    C) all Arctic mammals use sea ice for the same reason.

    D) all Arctic mammals struggle when the availability of sea ice decreases.

Babies and their Senses

The greatest changes in sensory, motor, and perceptual development happen in the first two years of life. When babies are first born, most of their senses operate in a similar way to those of adults. For example, babies are able to hear before they are born; studies show that babies turn toward the sound of their mothers' voices just minutes after being born, indicating they recognize the mother's voice from their time in the womb.

The exception to this rule is vision. A baby's vision changes significantly in its first year of life; initially it has a range of vision of only 8 – 12 inches and no depth perception. As a result, infants rely primarily on hearing; vision does not become the dominant sense until around the age of twelve months. Babies also prefer faces to other objects. This preference, along with their limited vision range, means that their sight is initially focused on their caregiver.

38. Which of the following senses do babies primarily rely on?

    A) vision

    B) hearing

    C) touch

    D) smell

39. Which of the following best describes the mode of the passage?

    A) expository

    B) narrative

    C) persuasive

    D) descriptive

40. Which of the following is a concise summary of the passage?

    A) Babies have no depth perception until twelve months, which is why they focus only on their caregivers' faces.

    B) Babies can recognize their mothers' voices when born, so they initially rely primarily on their sense of hearing.

    C) Babies have senses similar to those of adults except for their sense of sight, which doesn't fully develop until twelve months.

    D) Babies' senses go through many changes in the first year of their lives.

LISTENING

Please visit https://www.triviumtestprep.com/toefl-listening to listen to the recorded lectures for the practice tests.

Dialogue

DIRECTIONS: Listen to the dialogue, then answer the questions.

Raul and Mae are talking about their experiences at different study groups.

1. On which two days does Mae go to study groups?

   A) Mondays and Wednesdays

   B) Mondays and Sundays

   C) Wednesdays and Saturdays

   D) Wednesdays and Sundays

2. How do the study groups help Mae?

   A) by reviewing classmates' notes

   B) by listening to the TA re-read the lecture

   C) through discussion and asking questions

   D) through peer-reviewing essays with her classmates

3. Why doesn't Mae ask questions in class?

   A) She doesn't go to class.

   B) She is embarrassed to ask questions.

   C) She can't hear the professor.

   D) She prefers to listen.

4. What is one problem Mae and Raul have with Professor Roberts?

   A) He talks too fast.

   B) He doesn't answer questions.

   C) He is not approachable.

   D) He does not keep office hours.

5. On which two days does Raul go to study groups?

   A) Sunday and Monday

   B) Monday and Wednesday

   C) Wednesday and Saturday

   D) Saturday and Sunday

6. What score did Mae get on the midterm?

   A) A

   B) A-

   C) B+

   D) B

7. What is Raul's perspective on the study groups he attends?

   A) He finds them very helpful because he enjoys the discussion.

   B) He thinks the TA is a better teacher than the professor

   C) He does not find them useful because he knows more than the other students.

   D) He does not usually go often enough to find them enriching.

8. Which study groups are run by a TA?

   A) Saturday morning and Sunday night

   B) Sunday night and Monday night

   C) Monday night and Wednesday night

   D) Wednesday night and Saturday morning

9. At what two times does the Monday night study group meet?

   A) 6:00 and 6:30

   B) 6:15 and 6:45

   C) 6:30 and 7:00

   D) 7:00 and 7:30

10. How many students *usually* attend the Monday night study group?

    A) three to ten

    B) ten to twelve

    C) fifteen to twenty

    D) twenty-five to thirty

Lecture One

DIRECTIONS: Listen to the lecture, then answer the questions.

11. What is the lecture mainly about?

    A) the need for people in communities to maintain a social contract

    B) the difference between public property and private property

    C) the definition of public property and the challenges related to it

    D) the laws to protect public property and how they are effective

12. Why does the professor mention state university dormitories and dining halls?

    A) to illustrate how taxes can maintain public property

    B) to show that no single individual owns a state university

    C) to provide examples of debates over what qualifies as public property

    D) to explain access restrictions on certain types of public property

13. Why do some people qualify for "in-state tuition" rates?

    A) They have paid taxes for the support of the university system.

    B) They are the only people the university was designed to benefit.

    C) They are willing to use publicly owned facilities.

    D) They have qualified based on criteria set forth by the state.

14. Why does the professor mention "bandit signs"?

    A) to illustrate how some people take advantage of private property

    B) to emphasize multiple opinions about the appropriate use of public property

    C) to explain the way businesses and individuals have similar interests related to public property

    D) to highlight the need for public entities to increase enforcement of laws protecting private property

15. According to the professor, who owns public property?

    A) a single individual

    B) a group or entity

    C) all taxpayers in a country

    D) state university systems

16. What can be inferred about public property based on the lecture?

    A) It is a clearly outlined space that the public understands well.

    B) It requires governments to assert authority over property owners.

    C) It is not as important to our society as private property.

    D) It is a subject of debate in many local communities.

17. According to the professor, what is the land between the street and people's homes called?

    A) the easement

    B) an ordinance

    C) an access point

    D) a social contract

18. What is the professor implying when she says, "This might lead them to place cones, trees, large rocks, or other items either in the street or on the easement"?

    A) Public property relies on taking land away from individuals.

    B) Local governments don't adequately address parking issues.

    C) Some people confuse public property with private property.

    D) People have the right to maintain public streets as they see fit.

19. Why is compromise necessary with public property?

A) People are selfish and don't understand public property.

B) Governments limit how involved they get in public property issues.

C) The line between public and private property isn't always clear.

D) The social contract agreement doesn't help with matters of public property.

20. What is the professor explaining when she says, "For example, a person can't decide to open a business in the middle of a street or keep livestock on a public sidewalk"?

A) the overall purpose of public property

B) the limits on use of public property

C) the way public property benefits all

D) the confusion over what public property is

Lecture Two

DIRECTIONS: Listen to the lecture, then answer the questions.

21. What is the main purpose of the lecture?

A) to explain how to react to a performance art piece

B) to describe what is meant by performance art

C) to explain the interaction between audience and artist during a performance

D) to explain how a thoughtful performance makes us question the world around us

22. Why does the professor have a special appreciation for performance art?

A) She has seen many performances.

B) She is a professor of art history.

C) She is a performance artist.

D) She has strong opinions on the art form.

23. Which element is necessary in order for something to be considered performance art?

A) a live performance

B) a video or song

C) an artistic intervention

D) an audience

24. What element of a performance can the artist NOT control?

A) the reaction of the audience

B) the length of the piece

C) the types of materials used

D) the participation of others

25. Why does the professor mention "a flower or a rainbow"?

A) to illustrate examples of performance art

B) to provide nonexamples of performance art

C) to describe the natural beauty upon which performance art draws

D) to show that some performance art does not require an artist

26. According to the professor, in which case might the performance artist not be in attendance while his or her piece is presented to an audience?

A) The piece is made in collaboration with other artists.

B) The piece does not contain all three necessary elements.

C) The piece is meant to be viewed by only a select few people.

D) The piece is presented in a pre-recorded video format.

27. Why does the professor mention the art of H.A. Schult?

A) to give an example of a performance artist with no audience

B) to show the way performance art encourages thought and questioning

C) to emphasize the problem of performance art in generating a lot of garbage

D) to explain that performance artists most often rely on very large-scale works

28. Why does the professor refer to the performance at the conference hosted on campus last year?

   A) to explain that performance art is often viewed at conferences

   B) to suggest that performance art requires careful planning

   C) to show that performance art can make audiences uncomfortable

   D) to explain that performance art is targeted to a very specific person

29. According to the professor, why might the audience want to become involved in a performance art piece?

   A) They think the performers are in danger.

   B) They begin to evaluate their society.

   C) They want to help the artwork be completed.

   D) They are unaware of their role as an audience.

30. What can be inferred about the professor when she says the following?

"While we may look at a beautiful painting by Rembrandt and think 'that's beautiful,' it doesn't necessarily make us question society or the world around us. Performance art, when done well, almost always does this."

   A) The professor believes visual arts have no value in society.

   B) The professor wants students to question the beauty of paintings.

   C) The professor sees performance art as having qualities other arts lack.

   D) The professor believes that performance art is superior to all other art forms.

WRITING

There are two tasks on the Writing test. For the first task, you must read a passage and listen to a lecture on a certain subject. Then write a response answering a question based on what you read and heard.

On the second task, you will respond to a question drawing on your own knowledge and opinions.

Writing Based on Reading and Listening

DIRECTIONS: Read the text below. Then, visit https://www.triviumtestprep.com/toefl-listening. Scroll down to find the relevant recording, and click to listen to the accompanying lecture. You may take notes on the lecture.

Summarize the points made in the lecture, being sure to explain how they respond to specific points made in the reading passage. You will have twenty minutes to write your response. A typical response should be about 150 – 225 words long.

ECOTOURISM: A BENEFICIAL PRACTICE

Our world is full of enchanting places: the Colosseum, the Grand Canyon, Yellowstone National Park. Increasingly, there is concern in preserving these global treasures for future generations. One viable solution is ecotourism.

Ecotourism is a booming global industry. Ecotourists visit areas of cultural and environmental interest. They promote conservation and minimize human impacts. Ecotourism can have a positive effect on our world and allow global citizens to continue to enjoy sites of interest.

First of all, ecotourism increases awareness of the need to preserve important places. Visitors who take an ecotourist expedition to the Brazilian rainforest, for example, can learn about challenges like deforestation, urbanization, and resource production. Ecotourism also promotes conservation of historic sites. Many historic buildings from the Alamo to the Eiffel Tower need constant human intervention to remain in good condition for visitors.

Secondly, ecotourism has tangible financial benefits for local populations and tourist sites. Visitors to Mayan or Aztec ruins, for instance, might purchase locally made items from people indigenous to these communities, providing an important influx of capital into the local economy.

Lastly, a properly conducted ecotourist visit can increase global understanding. It is vitally important for people from all parts of the world to recognize and respect multiple cultural traditions. One important principle of ecotourism is helping visitors to a community have an authentic experience. That principle ensures a broader awareness of the environmental, political, and social climate of the host site.

Independent Writing

DIRECTIONS: Read the following prompt. Then, write an essay responding to the question. Use your own experience, ideas, and opinions to develop your response.

You have thirty minutes to plan, write, and revise your essay.

E-CIGARETTES

The rise in popularity of e-cigarettes has reduced the overall smoking rate according to government health agencies. Many people believe the new technology has helped smokers quit traditional tobacco cigarettes. However, others raise concerns about the appeal of e-cigarettes to young people and advocate government regulation of e-cigarettes to prevent negative side effects of their use on a new generation of smokers.

Should e-cigarettes be regulated by the government?

In your essay, take a position on this question. Give reasons for your answer and include any relevant examples from your own knowledge or experience.

ANSWER KEY

READING

1. **A) is correct.** The passage indicates that a snakes' "intricate diamonds, stripes, and swirls help the animals hide from predators, but perhaps most importantly (for us humans, anyway), the markings can also indicate whether the snake is venomous."

2. **B) is correct.** The final paragraph of the passage states that the two species "frequently [share] a habitat" and that a "predatory hawk or eagle, usually hunting from high in the sky, can't tell the difference between the two species, and so the kingsnake gets passed over and lives another day."

3. **D) is correct.** This summary captures the main ideas of each paragraph.

4. **C) is correct.** The first paragraph states that "while it might seem counterintuitive for a venomous snake to stand out in bright red or blue, that fancy costume tells any nearby predator that approaching him would be a bad idea." The coral snake's markings do not allow it to hide from predators but rather to "ward [them] off."

5. **A) is correct.** The passage states that "intricate diamonds, stripes, and swirls help the animals hide from predators," implying that these markings are complex enough

to allow the animals to blend in with their surroundings.

6. **C) is correct.** The second paragraph states that "the scarlet kingsnake, for example, has very similar markings to the venomous coral snake with whom it frequently shares a habitat. However, the kingsnake is actually nonvenomous."

7.

most accurate site for taking temperature	rectum
most common site for taking temperature	mouth
acceptable site for taking temperature	temporal artery

8. **B), C), D) are correct.** These details are all stated in the passage. The passage states that "the most common way people measure body temperature is orally," or through the mouth. It later mentions that "when a person can't breathe through his nose, he won't be able to keep his mouth closed long enough to get an accurate reading." In the same paragraph, the author writes, "using the rectum also has the added benefit of providing a much more accurate reading than other locations can provide."

9. **B) is correct.** In the first paragraph, the author writes, "But what's the best way to get an accurate reading? The answer depends on the situation." She then goes on to describe various options and their applications.

10. **B) is correct.** The author indicates that "the most common way people measure body temperature is orally" but that "there are many situations...when measuring temperature orally isn't an option." She then goes on to describe these situations in the second and third paragraphs.

11. **A) is correct.** The final paragraph states that "agitated patients...won't be able to sit still long enough for an accurate reading." The reader can infer that an agitated patient is a patient who is visibly upset, annoyed, or uncomfortable.

12. **A) is correct.** The second paragraph of the passage states that "using the rectum also has the added benefit of providing a much more accurate reading than other locations can provide."

13. **D) is correct.** The author writes, "The chemical elements in water, hydrogen and oxygen, are some of the most abundant elements in the universe. Astronomers see the signature of water in giant molecular clouds between the stars, in disks of material that represent newborn planetary systems, and in the atmospheres of giant planets orbiting other stars."

14. **A) is correct.** The author writes, "There are several worlds thought to possess liquid water beneath their surfaces, and many more that have water in the form of ice or vapor."

15. **B) is correct.** This excerpt illustrates the fact that water is available across the solar system in various forms.

16. **B) is correct.** The author writes, "Understanding the distribution of water in our solar system tells us a great deal about how the planets, moons, comets and other bodies formed 4.5 billion years ago from the disk of gas and dust that surrounded our sun."

17. **A) is correct.** The author writes that there are "three ingredients needed for life as we know it: liquid water, essential chemical elements for biological processes, and sources of energy that could be used by living things."

18. **D) is correct.** The author writes that the "'frost line'...is the approximate distance from the sun at which the ice on most comets begins to melt and become 'active.'" This implies that, outside this line, water begins to freeze.

19. **B) is correct.** The author writes that because "it was too hot in the solar system's early days for water to condense into liquid or ice on the inner planets...it had to be delivered—possibly by comets and water-bearing asteroids."

20. **D) is correct.** The author writes that the "brilliant spray" of water melting from the surface of comets "releases water ice, vapor, dust and other chemicals, which are thought to form the bedrock of most worlds of the frigid outer solar system." This suggests that the bedrock is the base, or foundation, of these outer worlds.

21. **C) is correct.** The passage and the table both indicate that numerous bodies in our solar system, including the moons of Jupiter and Saturn, show evidence of water.

22. **C) is correct.** This excerpt lists some of the ingredients that form the foundations of new worlds.

23.

MUSICIANS	WRITERS
Ella Fitzgerald	F. Scott Fitzgerald
Duke Ellington	
Bessie Smith	
Louis Armstrong	

24. **B) is correct.** The author writes that "jazz music was played by and for a more expressive and freed populace than the United States had previously seen." In addition to "the emergence of the flapper," the 1920s saw "the explosion of African American art

and culture now known as the Harlem Renaissance."

25. **A) is correct.** The author writes that "jazz music was played by and for a more expressive and freed populace than the United States had previously seen." In addition to "the emergence of the flapper," the 1920s saw "the explosion of African American art and culture now known as the Harlem Renaissance."

26. **C) is correct.** The author opens the passage saying, "In recent decades, jazz has been associated with New Orleans and festivals like Mardi Gras, but in the 1920s, jazz was a booming trend whose influence reached into many aspects of American culture." He then goes on to elaborate on what these movements were.

27. **B) is correct.** At the end of the first paragraph, the author writes, "Ella Fitzgerald, for example, moved from Virginia to New York City to begin her much-lauded singing career, and jazz pioneer Louis Armstrong got his big break in Chicago."

28. **C) is correct.** The author writes that "jazz music was played by and for a more expressive and freed populace than the United States had previously seen." In addition to "the emergence of the flapper," the 1920s saw "the explosion of African American art and culture now known as the Harlem Renaissance."

29. **D) is correct.** The author writes that "the melt season has grown longer and the average extent of Arctic sea ice has diminished, changing the game for many Arctic marine mammals."

30. **B) is correct.** The author writes that "many human communities want answers about the current status and future of Arctic marine mammals, including...indigenous people whose traditional ways of subsistence are intertwined with the fate of species such as ice seals, narwhals, walruses and polar bears." This implies that the survival of these groups depends on the survival of these animal species.

31. **D) is correct.** The author quotes one scientist as saying, "mainly, just continuing daily coverage is what's important for the long-term monitoring of habitat changes."

32. **D) is correct.** This excerpt implies that the survival of Arctic species is in jeopardy as a result of longer melting seasons and decreased sea ice extent.

33. **D) is correct.** The author writes that "there are many unknowns...about how their fragile habitat will evolve in a warming world." This implies that the habitat is at risk due to the changes in the earth's temperature.

34. **D) is correct.** The author writes, "Using daily sea ice concentration data from the satellite record, he [Stern] calculated changes in the dates of the beginning of the melt season in spring and the start of the fall freeze-up from 1979 to 2013. He found that, in all regions but one, the melt season had grown longer (mostly by five to ten weeks, and by twenty weeks in one region)."

35. **C) is correct.** The author indicates that the "earlier retreat of sea ice opens up new habitats," implying the retreat of sea ice is its recession, or backing off, due to melting.

36. **D) is correct.** The author indicates that "monitoring" the "daily coverage" of sea ice is necessary to understanding how the expansion and recession of sea ice will shape habitats over time.

37. **A) is correct.** The author states that, unlike other Arctic species, "in the case of Arctic whales, the changes in sea ice might benefit their populations, at least in the short term: the loss and earlier retreat of sea ice opens up new habitats and, in some areas of the Arctic, has also led to an increase in food production and the length of their feeding season."

38. **B) is correct.** The passage states that "infants rely primarily on hearing."

39. **A) is correct.** The passage explains how a baby's senses develop and allow it to interact with the world.

40. C) is correct. The passage states that babies'
senses are much like those of their adult
counterparts with the exception of their
vision, which develops later.

LISTENING

Dialogue

Raul and Mae are talking about their experiences at different study groups.

Raul: Do you go to a philosophy study group?

Mae: Yeah; I go to the one on Wednesday nights in Room B 100 and the one on Monday nights in Room C 120.

Raul: Do they help you? What did you score on the midterm exam?

Mae: Well...it helps me to talk about different philosophers with other people. Since the class is mostly lecture, the study groups help me through the discussion. I can also ask questions. I feel too embarrassed to ask questions in class. Plus...he talks so fast! I got a B+ on the midterm, though.

Raul: Professor Roberts definitely speaks pretty fast. I've been going to the study group on Sunday night... and sometimes the one on Saturday morning. Neither are very good.

Mae: Why not? Do the TAs run them...or someone else?

Raul: The one on Sunday nights is run by a TA. It's just that it doesn't really help me. It's mostly the same as the class lecture. The one on Saturday mornings is just a group of students. Most of the time, I know more than they do about philosophy!

Mae: You should try the Monday night study group. It meets at either 6:30 or 7:00, depending on what time the TA can get there that week. Usually, anywhere from three to ten people come; most times, there are at least five of us. But I'm sure they would welcome more...especially if you know what you are talking about when it comes to philosophy!

Raul: I wouldn't say I *always* know what I'm talking about!

1. **A) is correct.** Mae says, "I go to the one on Wednesday nights in Room B 100 and the one on Monday nights in Room C 120."

2. **C) is correct.** Mae says, "Since the class is mostly lecture, the study groups help me through discussion. I can also ask questions."

3. **B) is correct.** Mae says, "I feel too embarrassed to ask questions in class."

4. **A) is correct.** About Professor Roberts, Mae says, "he talks so fast!" Raul adds, "Professor Roberts definitely speaks pretty fast."

5. **D) is correct.** Raul says, "I've been going to the study group on Sunday night...and sometimes the one on Saturday morning."

6. **C) is correct.** Mae says, "I got a B+ on the midterm, though."

7. **C) is correct.** Raul says, "The one on Sunday nights is run by a TA. It's just that it doesn't really help me. It's mostly the same as the class lecture. The one on Saturday mornings is just a group of students. Most of the time, I know more than they do about philosophy!"

8. **B) is correct.** Mae says, "You should try the Monday night study group. It meets at either 6:30 or 7:00, depending on what time the TA can get there that week." Raul says, "The one on Sunday nights is run by a TA." Mae mentions going to a group on Wednesday nights, but it is not clear if a TA runs that group. Raul states, "a group on Saturday mornings is just a group of students"—with no TA.

9. **C) is correct.** Mae says, "It meets at either 6:30 or 7:00."

10. A) is correct. Mae says, "Usually, anywhere from three to ten people come; most times, there are at least five of us."

Lecture One

So, we've been talking about the way society divides land into sections or private property for individuals to use. If you'll remember, they use this property for a variety of things: a place to live, farm, keep livestock, open a business, rent out property to others, and so forth. However, not everything in our society is private property.

We also, of course, have public property, which includes parks, roads, libraries, sewers, and other publicly owned land and facilities. These are owned not by a single individual but by another entity such as a state, county, city, or other group. Such public property exists to benefit all, and no single individual can claim ownership.

While a single individual doesn't own public property and the goal is for the property to benefit all people in a location, this doesn't mean that anyone can claim or use the property at will. For example, a public street can only be used for certain purposes, such as driving a motor vehicle or bicycle. A resident of a city has a right to access the public street, but not for *any* purpose. For example, a person can't decide to open a business in the middle of a street or keep livestock on a public sidewalk.

Public property is typically funded through taxation. Because a particular entity is funded only by the taxation of individuals within that entity, it might limit access to those outside it. Consider a public university. No single individual owns the university, but there may be certain restrictions on access. For example, only students might be allowed to access certain facilities like dormitories and dining halls.

Furthermore, the university might provide benefits to those who live within the particular state, like reduced tuition costs. Such "in-state tuition" policies are typically implemented because the residents of that state are already being taxed in support of the university system. So, they have theoretically already "prepaid" a portion of the tuition. Non-residents of the state have not been taxed and are thus asked to pay a higher tuition rate.

Sometimes the use of public property is contested. In some cities and counties, laws exist to prevent certain actions on public property. For example, city ordinances in most communities prohibit the use of what are sometimes called "bandit signs," small advertisements that are staked into an esplanade or along the side of roadways. While businesses may argue that the land is public property and should be open to multiple uses such as marketing, local residents might not want to look at such signs in their communities and might push for laws against them.

Parking is another big issue related to public property. Sometimes people do things to restrict the public's ability to park on streets or the easement—the strip of land between the road and the sidewalk in front of some homes. Homeowners argue that they don't want this public area in front of their home full of cars, or they want to reserve the space for their own cars. So they place cones, trees, large rocks, or other items in the street or on the easement. While some cities have ordinances against this, others do not.

As you can see, the line between private property and public property isn't always crystal clear. That means that part of our social contract, or agreement with others to cooperate for certain benefits, will almost always require compromise.

11. **C) is correct.** The professor's lecture is primarily about how "we also, of course, have public property" in addition to private property. Further, there are challenges with this since "sometimes use of public property is contested."

12. **D) is correct.** The professor uses state university dorms and dining halls to explain access restrictions. She says, "Consider a public university. No single individual owns the university, but there may be certain restrictions on access. For example, only students might be allowed to access certain facilities like dormitories and dining halls."

13. **A) is correct.** The professor states that residents in a state "have theoretically already 'prepaid' a portion of the tuition."

14. **B) is correct.** This shows two differing opinions: "While businesses may argue that the land is public property and should be open to multiple uses such as marketing, local residents might not want to look at such signs in their communities."

15. **B) is correct.** According to the professor, public property is owned "by another entity such as a state, county, city, or other group."

16. **D) is correct.** Based on the lecture, especially the parts about contested issues (bandit signs, parking, and so forth), we can infer that the definition and use of "public property" are under debate in many communities.

17. **A) is correct.** According to the lecture, the easement is "the strip of land between the road and the sidewalk in front of some homes."

18. **C) is correct.** The professor had previously said that these areas are public property but some individuals restrict access. So some people are confusing public and private properties. According to the professor, "Homeowners argue that they don't want this public area in front of their home full of cars, or they want to reserve the space for their own cars. So they place cones, trees, large rocks, or other items in the street or on the easement."

19. **C) is correct.** The professor mentions this at the end of the lecture in that "the line between private property and public property isn't always crystal clear." So sometimes, compromise is needed.

20. **B) is correct.** This sentence explains that while "a resident has a right to access the public street," he or she cannot access it for "*any* purpose."

Lecture Two

When studying contemporary arts, we often focus on visual arts, like painting and sculpture. However, this is most certainly not the only type of contemporary art. One facet of the art world that we have yet to explore is close to my own heart since I am a practitioner: performance art.

So, what is performance art? The textbooks and even the artists themselves have myriad definitions of this unique medium. One common understanding of performance art is "art performed live." But to me, this doesn't quite go far enough. Simply watching someone paint or sculpt isn't really performance art.

I'd say for something to qualify as performance art it needs three elements: an artist, an audience, and a relationship between the two.

First, there must be an artist. A sunset, for example, might be extremely beautiful, but it isn't created or conceived by an artist in the strictest sense, so it doesn't qualify. Same with a flower or a rainbow. Of course, the artist doesn't need to be present during the performance. He or she might create a video or song or even an artistic intervention—a purposeful change in an environment, audience, or situation. This might then be presented to the audience without the artist physically present or physically performing the piece. However, the artist is still *present* in the piece since it is an extension of the artist.

Second, there must be an audience of some sort. Performance art cannot exist in a vacuum or sit around in a museum's dusty storage closet. It must be seen, usually by a live audience.

And of course, performance art must involve some sort of dynamic between artist and audience. In some performance art pieces, the audience becomes part of the performance and participates in the piece. In others, the audience simply observes and reacts. Like any artistic endeavor, the perspective of each individual observer will be distinct. However, the artist often hopes to call the audience's attention to a societal issue. One famous German artist, named H.A. Schult, creates large installations of people and buildings made entirely out of garbage. His motive is to point out the massive amount of waste that humans create. Of course, he cannot control the reaction of any particular audience. Some observers might just see something unique and beautiful.

Sometimes the relationship between the artist and the audience can be a very complex one. Performance art pieces are often designed to make an audience question its values or the values of the society in which it lives. At a performance art conference we hosted on campus last year, I saw an artist who smashed a bunch of cell phones and computers with a hammer. Everyone in the audience gasped. It was quite a spectacle, since some of the devices were brand new! The point was to make the audience evaluate an overdependence on technology, which many found uncomfortable.

Audiences are often meant to feel uncomfortable at performance art events, though. Some artists even experiment with whether or not the audience will intervene by creating a situation in which it appears the artist or performers are in imminent danger. Since they usually understand that they should not interact with the artwork in progress, audiences then have to fight an urge to help.

One of the best things about performance art is the way it encourages thought in the observer. While we may look at a beautiful painting by Rembrandt and think "that's beautiful," it doesn't necessarily make us question society or the world around us. Performance art, when done well, almost always does this.

21. **B) is correct.** The lecture aims primarily to answer the question, "So, what is performance art?"

22. **C) is correct.** The professor says that performance art is "close to [her] own heart since [she] is a practitioner."

23. **D) is correct.** The professor says, "I'd say for something to qualify as performance art it has to involve three elements: an artist, an audience, and a relationship between the two."

24. **A) is correct.** The professor states that the performance artists "cannot control the reaction of any particular audience."

25. **B) is correct.** The professor explains that like a flower or rainbow, "a sunset...isn't created or conceived by an artist in the strictest sense, so it doesn't qualify" as performance art.

26. **D) is correct.** The professor states, "Of course, the artist need not be present during the performance. He or she might create a video or song or even an artistic intervention."

27. **B) is correct.** Schult is presented as an example of the way that "the artist often hopes to call the audience's attention to a societal issue."

28. **C) is correct.** The professor states, "The point was to make the audience evaluate an overdependence on technology, which many found uncomfortable." The specific example is used to show how audiences can

sometimes feel uncomfortable when viewing performance art.

29. **A) is correct.** The professor explains, "Some artists even experiment with whether or not the audience will intervene by creating a situation in which it appears the artist or performers are in imminent danger."

30. **C) is correct.** This is a reasonable inference because the professor directly compares visual art in a Rembrandt painting to performance art. While the painting might be beautiful, it doesn't "make us question society or the world around us." However, unlike visual art, performance art *does* accomplish this.

WRITING

Ecotourism is often called a solution to the problem of global habitat destruction. Unfortunately, despite the best of intentions, ecotourism typically does more harm than good. It is simply another way that the wealthy exploit the environments and lives of the less fortunate.

Proponents of ecotourism say that it promotes a conservation mindset, but human impacts on vulnerable places are often negative. Any human intervention into an ecosystem—even a hike on a trail or a boat ride on a river—has an environmental impact. Usually this impact harms native wildlife and flora. Humans might go into a site with the best of intentions, but their very presence—in a forest, on a lake, or on a savannah—disrupts the natural events of that ecosystem.

Furthermore, the humans living in these locations are harmed by ecotourism. Many of these popular ecotourist sites are located in developing countries with significant indigenous populations. These communities are trying to maintain their way of life without the interference of outside forces. A group of tourists with motor vehicles and smartphones driving into a remote village is a nuisance. They put a strain on local resources, like food and water, which might already be limited. Additionally, such tourists often lack skills in the local language and thus remain unable to communicate with the host community.

Depending on the particular tour guide or group, there is the risk that native people might also be portrayed as "curiosities" for visitors. Instead of promoting cultural understanding and awareness, this exploitation perpetuates the racist notion that indigenous groups are "primitive" or "backward." In fact, most indigenous populations have very advanced social and religious practices that are frequently misunderstood by tourists who lack the background to fully appreciate them.

Finally, ecotourist adventures, like almost all tourism, depend on fossil fuels to transport people from place to place. Air travel causes significant environmental pollution. Since ecotourist destinations are often thousands of miles away from the home nation of the tourist, these flights are long, so they consume a huge amount of jet fuel. Even after the destination country is reached, local sites are most often visited by tourists via automobile or boat, both of which are gasoline-powered vehicles that further pollute the environment.

When we examine all the evidence related to the practice of ecotourism, it becomes clear that these trips are really just a way of making rich people feel like they are doing something "good," when really they are exploiting the very people and habitats that their trips are designed to "help." It is rare that people who venture to such locations with good intentions actually make any type of positive impact in the long run. Most go home and continue with their daily lives: driving large automobiles that burn fossil fuels, consuming more than their fair share of resources, and contributing to the further degradation of our planet.

Writing Based on Reading and Listening: Sample Student Response

Summarize the points made in the lecture, being sure to explain how they respond to specific points made in the reading passage.

The lecture explains how ecotourism is not the great solution to environmental destruction that the text makes it appear to be.

First of all, the lecture points out that any human involvement in an ecosystem has negative impacts. This stands in contrast to the point made in the text that ecotourism leads to preservation or conservation of important global sites. While people who visit such locations might think they are helping, the lecture argues that they are actually harming the area simply by being there and disturbing the plants and animals in the ecosystem.

Secondly, the lecture makes clear that ecotourism harms local populations. It can disrupt the way of life for native peoples and may even put these individuals "on display" for tourists, which can lead to negative stereotypes. This contrasts with the point in the text that ecotourism might have benefits for local populations in the way it might help the local economy.

Lastly, the lecture explains that any type of tourism, like ecotourism, causes environmental problems because of the use of fossil fuels. These negative environmental impacts are not mentioned in the text, which sees broader global understanding of other cultures as one of the benefits of this tourism.

Independent Writing: Sample Student Response

The number of youth smoking traditional cigarettes has never been lower. But electronic cigarettes (e-cigarettes) have skyrocketed in popularity. E-cigarettes should be regulated by the government to prevent youth from smoking since the long-term effects of e-cig use are unknown, youth are still becoming addicted to nicotine, and e-cigs could be a gateway to traditional smoking.

Smoking has long been a way for young people to feel cool or sophisticated. Although traditional smoking is no longer considered cool, the use of e-cigarettes, or vaping, is more and more widely accepted. E-cigarettes are not regulated by the government, so there are no restrictions on their advertisement. This allows e-cig companies to reach youth through a wide range of media. Furthermore, the design of e-cigs and the variety of flavors make them especially appealing to youth.

This is particularly concerning as the long-term effects of vaping are not yet known. The technology is too new to have been studied adequately. The government must study a drug for years before it can become available to the general public. Yet this device that delivers a highly addictive substance is unregulated. It may be true that e-cigarettes are healthier for smokers than traditional cigarettes, but we still do not know the impact on young people.

In addition, we do know that nicotine is a highly addictive drug. Nicotine use could alter the brain chemistry of young people. Even if vaping does not become a gateway to hard drug use, it does make the leap to traditional smoking much more likely.

The government has a responsibility to protect the public's health: regulation is needed to protect the youth and help a generation live longer, healthier lives.

5

PRACTICE TEST TWO

READING

DIRECTIONS: Read the passage and/or figure, and then answer the question.

Geography and its Sub-disciplines

In its most basic form, geography is the study of space; more specifically, it studies the physical space of the earth and the ways in which it interacts with, shapes, and is shaped by its habitants. Geographers look at the world from a spatial perspective. This means that at the center of all geographic study is the question, *where?* For geographers, the *where* of any interaction, event, or development is a crucial element to understanding it.

This question of *where* can be asked in a variety of fields of study, so there are many sub-disciplines of geography. These can be organized into four main categories: 1) regional studies, which examine the characteristics of a particular place; 2) topical studies, which look at a single physical or human feature that impacts the whole world; 3) physical studies, which focus on the physical features of Earth; and 4) human studies, which examine the relationship between human activity and the environment.

1. Match the topic to the field of study it belongs to.

Regional Studies	
Topical Studies	
Physical Studies	
Human Studies	

- a study of volcanoes and volcanic rock
- scholarship on the global impact of ozone layer depletion
- research on the impact of agriculture on prairie habitats
- a comparison of the ecosystems of the Great Lakes in the Midwest

2. Which of the following is a concise summary of the passage?

A) The most important questions in geography are where an event or development took place.

B) Geography, which is the study of the physical space on Earth, can be broken down into four sub-disciplines.

C) Regional studies specialists study a single region or area.

D) Geography can be broken down into four sub-disciplines: regional studies, topical studies, physical studies, and human studies.

3. A researcher studying the relationship between farming and river systems would be engaged in which of the following geographical sub-disciplines?

   A) regional studies

   B) topical studies

   C) physical studies

   D) human studies

4. Which of the following best describes the mode of the passage?

   A) expository

   B) narrative

   C) persuasive

   D) descriptive

The US Civil War

It could be said that the great battle between the North and South we call the Civil War was a battle for individual identity. The states of the South had their own culture, one based on farming, independence, and the rights of both man and state to determine their own paths. Similarly, the North had forged its own identity as a center of centralized commerce and manufacturing. This clash of lifestyles was bound to create tension, and this tension was bound to lead to war. But people who try to sell you this narrative are wrong. The Civil War was not a battle of cultural identities—it was a battle about slavery. All other explanations for the war are either a direct consequence of the South's desire for wealth at the expense of her fellow man or a fanciful invention to cover up this sad portion of our nation's history. And it cannot be denied that this time in our past was very sad indeed.

5. What is the meaning of the word *fanciful* in the passage?

   A) complicated

   B) imaginative

   C) successful

   D) unfortunate

6. What is the main idea of the passage?

   A) The Civil War was the result of cultural differences between the North and South.

   B) The Civil War was caused by the South's reliance on slave labor.

   C) The North's use of commerce and manufacturing allowed it to win the war.

   D) The South's belief in the rights of man and state cost the war.

7. What is the author's primary purpose in writing this essay?

   A) to convince readers that slavery was the main cause of the Civil War

   B) to illustrate the cultural differences between the North and the South before the Civil War

   C. to persuade readers that the North deserved to win the Civil War

   D. to demonstrate that the history of the Civil War is too complicated to be understood clearly

The Truth About Weight Loss

We've been told for years that the recipe for weight loss is fewer calories in than calories out. In other words, eat less and exercise more, and your body will take care of the rest. As many of those who've tried to diet can attest, this edict doesn't always produce results. If you're one of those folks, you might have felt that you just weren't doing it right—that the failure was all your fault.

However, several new studies released this year have suggested that it might not be your fault at all. For example, a study of people who'd lost a high percentage of their body weight (>17%) in a short period of time found that they could not physically maintain their new weight. Scientists measured their resting metabolic rate and found that they'd need to consume only a few hundred calories a day to meet their metabolic needs. Basically, their bodies were in starvation mode and seemed to desperately hang on to each and every calorie. Eating even a single healthy, well-balanced meal a day would cause these subjects to start packing back on the pounds.

Other studies have shown that factors like intestinal bacteria, distribution of body fat, and hormone levels can affect the manner in which our bodies process calories. There's also the fact that it's actually quite difficult to measure the number of calories consumed during a particular meal and the number used while exercising.

8. Which of the following would be the best summary statement to conclude the passage?

   A) It turns out that conventional dieting wisdom doesn't capture the whole picture of how our bodies function.

   B) Still, counting calories and tracking exercise is a good idea if you want to lose weight.

   C) In conclusion, it's important to lose weight responsibly: losing too much weight at once can negatively impact the body.

   D) It's easy to see that diets don't work, so we should focus less on weight loss and more on overall health.

9. Which type of argument is used in the passage?

   A) emotional argument

   B) appeal to authority

   C) specific evidence

   D) rhetorical questioning

10. Which of the following would weaken the author's argument?

   A) a new diet pill from a pharmaceutical company that promises to help patients lose weight by changing intestinal bacteria

   B) the personal experience of a man who was able to lose a significant amount of weight by taking in fewer calories than he used

   C) a study showing that people in different geographic locations lose different amounts of weight when on the same diet

   D) a study showing that people often misreport their food intake when part of a scientific study on weight loss

The Global Effects of Nuclear War

The following passage is an excerpt from the introduction to the United States Arms Control and Disarmament Agency's publication, Worldwide Effects of Nuclear War: Some Perspectives, *1975.*

It has now been two decades since the introduction of thermonuclear fusion weapons into the military inventories of the great powers, and more than a decade since the United States, Great Britain, and the Soviet Union ceased to test nuclear weapons in the atmosphere. Today our understanding of the technology of thermonuclear weapons seems highly advanced, but our knowledge of the physical and biological consequences of nuclear war is continuously evolving.

Only recently, new light was shed on the subject in a study which the Arms Control and Disarmament Agency had asked the National Academy of Sciences to undertake. Previous studies had tended to focus very largely on radioactive fallout from a nuclear war; an important aspect of this new study was its inquiry into all possible consequences, including the effects of large-scale nuclear detonations on the ozone layer which helps protect life on earth from the sun's ultraviolet radiations. Assuming a total detonation of 10,000 megatons—a large-scale but less than total nuclear "exchange," as one would say in the dehumanizing jargon of the strategists—it was concluded that as much as 30 – 70 percent of the ozone might be eliminated from the northern hemisphere (where a nuclear war would presumably take place) and as much as 20 – 40 percent from the southern hemisphere. Recovery would probably take about 3 – 10 years, but the Academy's study notes that long term global changes cannot be completely ruled out.

The reduced ozone concentrations would have a number of consequences outside the areas in which the detonations occurred. The Academy study notes, for example, that the resultant increase in ultraviolet would cause "prompt incapacitating cases of sunburn in the temperate zones and snow blindness in northern countries..."

Strange though it might seem, the increased ultraviolet radiation could also be accompanied by a drop in the average temperature. The size of the change is open to question, but the largest changes would probably occur at the higher latitudes, where crop production and ecological balances are sensitively dependent on the number of frost-free days and other factors related to average temperature. The Academy's study concluded that ozone changes due to nuclear war might decrease global surface temperatures by only negligible amounts or by as much as a few degrees. To calibrate the significance of this, the study mentioned that a cooling of even 1 degree centigrade would eliminate commercial wheat growing in Canada.

Thus, the possibility of a serious increase in ultraviolet radiation has been added to widespread radioactive fallout as a fearsome consequence of the large-scale use of nuclear weapons. And it is likely that we must reckon with still other complex and subtle processes, global in scope, which could seriously threaten the health of distant populations in the event of an all-out nuclear war.

Up to now, many of the important discoveries about nuclear weapon effects have been made not through deliberate scientific inquiry but by accident. And as the following historical examples show, there has been a series of surprises.

"Castle/Bravo" was the largest nuclear weapon ever detonated by the United States. Before it was set off at Bikini on February 28, 1954, it was expected to explode with an energy equivalent of about 8 million tons of TNT. Actually, it produced almost twice that explosive power—equivalent to 15 million tons of TNT.

If the power of the bomb was unexpected, so were the after-effects. About 6 hours after the explosion, a fine, sandy ash began to sprinkle the Japanese fishing vessel Lucky Dragon, some 90 miles downwind of the burst point, and Rongelap Atoll, 100 miles downwind. Though 40 to 50 miles away from the proscribed test area, the vessel's crew and the islanders received heavy doses of radiation from the weapon's "fallout"—the coral rock, soil, and other debris sucked up in the fireball and made intensively radioactive by the nuclear reaction. One radioactive isotope in the fallout, iodine-131, rapidly built up to serious concentration in the thyroid glands of the victims, particularly young Rongelapese children.

More than any other event in the decade of testing large nuclear weapons in the atmosphere, Castle/Bravo's unexpected contamination of 7,000 square miles of the Pacific Ocean dramatically illustrated how large-scale nuclear war could produce casualties on a colossal scale, far beyond the local effects of blast and fire alone.

11. What is the passage primarily concerned with?

A) describing the effects of large-scale detonations on the ozone layer

B) comparing an increase in ultraviolet radiation to an increase in radioactive fallout

C) explaining the aftereffects of the 1954 nuclear blast

D) providing facts about the consequences of a nuclear war

12. What would the author most likely recommend?

A) All countries should have information about the consequences of using nuclear weapons.

B) Americans should stop producing nuclear weapons.

C) All countries should stop testing nuclear weapons.

D) Research should continue on the historical examples of nuclear power.

13. In paragraph 2, what does the term *dehumanizing jargon* refer to?

    A) detonation of 10,000 megatons

    B) nuclear "exchange"

    C) large-scale detonation

    D) study of the Arms Control and Disarmament Agency

14. How is the author's attitude toward the past and potential future use of nuclear weapons best described?

    A) indifference

    B) urgency

    C) confusion

    D) despair

15. Which of the following best describes the organization of the passage?

    A) The problem of nuclear detonations and war is discussed; then, possible solutions are evaluated.

    B) The term *thermonuclear technology* is defined with scientific explanations.

    C) Descriptions are included of each nuclear detonation that occurred in the twentieth century.

    D) Research is explained with a series of results from scientific studies.

16. Why does the author note that "Castle/Bravo" was the largest nuclear weapon ever detonated by the United States?

    A) to show the unexpected power and after-effects of a detonated nuclear weapon

    B) to highlight the flaw in the view that nuclear weapons are sometimes necessary

    C) to identify the issue that led to the ban on nuclear weapons

    D) to illustrate the controversy over the significance of the detonation

17. The author puts quotation marks around the word *fallout* in the penultimate paragraph to emphasize that

    A) the lethal isotopes that fall with the bombs are invisible.

    B) the contamination from the detonation was unnoticed.

    C) the political upheaval caused by the detonation became the fallout.

    D) the euphemistic term *fallout* minimizes the horrific impact of the radioactive debris.

18. What is the meaning of the word *evolving* in paragraph 1?

    A) changing

    B) interpreting

    C) determining

    D) developing

19. What is the primary purpose of the first paragraph of the passage?

    A) to provide a statement about the current status of knowledge about nuclear war

    B) to identify the countries that have nuclear weapons

    C) to reassure the reader that no country is currently testing nuclear weapons

    D) to discuss the controversy over nuclear weapons

20. According to the passage, why do scientists believe that long-term global changes are a possible consequence of nuclear war?

    A) Recovery from nuclear detonation takes a long time.

    B) The northern hemisphere would be eliminated.

    C) The ozone layer would be damaged and ultraviolet radiation would increase.

    D) Widespread ecological imbalances would create panic.

All About Influenza

Influenza (also called the flu) has historically been one of the most common, and deadliest, human infections. While many people who contract the virus will recover, many others will not. Over the past 150 years, tens of millions of people have died from the flu, and millions more have been left with lingering complications such as secondary infections.

Although it's a common disease, the flu is not actually highly infectious, meaning it's relatively difficult to contract. The flu can only be transmitted when individuals come into direct contact with bodily fluids of people infected with the flu or when they are exposed to expelled aerosol particles (which result from coughing and sneezing). Because the viruses can only travel short distances as aerosol particles and will die within a few hours on hard surfaces, the virus can be contained with fairly simple health measures like hand washing and face masks.

However, the spread of the flu can only be contained when people are aware such measures need to be taken. One of the reasons the flu has historically been so deadly is the amount of time between when people become infectious and when they develop symptoms. Viral shedding—the process by which the body releases viruses that have been successfully reproducing during the infection—takes place two days after infection, while symptoms do not usually develop until the third day of infection. Thus, infected individuals have at least twenty-four hours in which they may unknowingly infect others.

21. What is the main idea of the passage?

    A) The flu is a deadly disease that's difficult to control because people become infectious before they show symptoms.

    B) For the flu to be transmitted, individuals must come in contact with bodily fluids from infected individuals.

    C) The spread of the flu is easy to contain because the viruses do not live long either as aerosol particles or on hard surfaces.

    D) The flu has killed tens of millions of people and can often cause deadly secondary infections.

22. Which of the following correctly describes the flu?

    A) The flu is easy to contract and always fatal.

    B) The flu is difficult to contract and always fatal.

    C) The flu is easy to contract and sometimes fatal.

    D) The flu is difficult to contract and sometimes fatal.

23. Why is the flu considered to not be highly infectious?

    A) Many people who get the flu will recover and have no lasting complications, so only a small number of people who become infected will die.

    B) The process of viral shedding takes two days, so infected individuals have enough time to implement simple health measures that stop the spread of the disease.

    C) The flu virus cannot travel far or live for long periods of time outside the human body, so its spread can easily be contained.

    D) Twenty-four hours is a relatively short period of time for the virus to spread among a population.

24. What is the meaning of the word *measures* in the last paragraph?

    A) a plan of action

    B) a standard unit

    C) an adequate amount

    D) a rhythmic movement

25. Which statement is NOT a detail from the passage?

A) Tens of millions of people have been killed by the flu virus.

B) There is typically a twenty-four-hour window during which individuals are infectious but not showing flu symptoms.

C) Viral shedding is the process by which people recover from the flu.

D) The flu can be transmitted by direct contact with bodily fluids from infected individuals or by exposure to aerosol particles.

26. What can the reader conclude from the passage?

A) Preemptively implementing health measures like hand washing and face masks could help stop the spread of the flu virus.

B) Doctors are not sure how the flu virus is transmitted, so they are unsure how to stop it from spreading.

C) The flu is dangerous because it is both deadly and highly infectious.

D) Individuals stop being infectious three days after they are infected.

Commensalism

The bacteria, fungi, insects, plants, and animals that live together in a habitat have evolved to share a pool of limited resources. They've competed for water, minerals, nutrients, sunlight, and space—sometimes for thousands or even millions of years. As these communities have evolved, the species in them have developed complex, long-term interspecies interactions known as symbiotic relationships.

Ecologists characterize these interactions based on whether each party benefits. In mutualism, both individuals benefit, while in synnecrosis, both organisms are harmed. A relationship where one individual benefits and the other is harmed is known as parasitism. Examples of these relationships can easily be seen in any ecosystem. Pollination, for example, is mutualistic—pollinators get nutrients from the flower, and the plant is able to reproduce—while tapeworms, which steal nutrients from their host, are parasitic.

There's yet another class of symbiosis that is controversial among scientists. As it's long been defined, commensalism is a relationship where one species benefits and the other is unaffected. But is it possible for two species to interact and for one to remain completely unaffected? Often, relationships described as commensal include one species that feeds on another species' leftovers; remoras, for instance, will attach themselves to sharks and eat the food particles they leave behind. It might seem like the shark gets nothing from the relationship, but a closer look will show that sharks in fact benefit from remoras, which clean the sharks' skin and remove parasites. In fact, many scientists claim that relationships currently described as commensal are just mutualistic or parasitic in ways that haven't been discovered yet.

27. What is the author's primary purpose in writing this essay?

A) to argue that commensalism isn't actually found in nature

B) to describe the many types of symbiotic relationships

C) to explain how competition for resources results in long-term interspecies relationships

D) to provide examples of the many different ways individual organisms interact

28. Which of the following is NOT a fact stated in the passage?

A) Mutualism is an interspecies relationship where both species benefit.

B) Synnecrosis is an interspecies relationship where both species are harmed.

C) The relationship between plants and pollinators is mutualistic.

D) The relationship between remoras and sharks is parasitic.

29. Epiphytes are plants that attach themselves to trees and derive nutrients from the air and surrounding debris. Sometimes, the weight of epiphytes can damage the trees on which they're growing. What is the relationship between epiphytes and their hosts?

A) mutualism

B) commensalism

C) parasitism

D) synnecrosis

30. Why is commensalism controversial among scientists?

A) Many scientists believe that an inter-species interaction where one species is unaffected does not exist.

B) Some scientists believe that relationships where one species feeds on the leftovers of another should be classified as parasit-ism.

C) Because remoras and sharks have a mutualistic relationship, no interactions should be classified as commensalism.

D) Only relationships among animal species should be classified as commensalism.

31. What is the meaning of the word *controversial* in the last paragraph?

A) debatable

B) objectionable

C) confusing

D) upsetting

32. What can the reader conclude from this passage about symbiotic relationships?

A) Scientists cannot decide how to classify symbiotic relationships among species.

B) Most interspecies interactions are par-asitic because most species do not get along.

C) If two species are involved in a parasitic relationship, one of the species will even-tually become extinct.

D) Symbiotic relationships evolve as the species that live in a community adapt to their environments and each other.

Hospital Nutrition

Providing adequate nutrition is one of the most important responsibilities of acute and long-term care facilities. Patients enter these facilities with a wide range of health issues from fractures and infections to dementia or cancer. Because the needs of every patient will be different, it's the task of every health care facility to ensure that patients receive the proper nutrition.

Patients, like all people, have two basic nutritional needs: they require macronutrients, the carbohydrates, fats, and proteins that provide energy; and micronutrients, which are the vitamins and elements the body needs to function properly. A good diet will provide the appropriate amount of macronutrients, or calories, to keep the patients energized and satiated without leading to weight gain while also providing necessary amounts of micronutrients. Such a diet will help patients remain comfortable and heal properly. A poor diet, on the other hand, can make recovery significantly more difficult.

The energy needs of patients can vary widely. Generally, energy needs are directly related to a person's weight and inversely related to age; it's also generally true that men require more calories than women. Thus, a thirty-five-year-old woman who weighs 135 pounds will require around 1800 calories a day, while an older woman would require fewer, and a heavier woman would require more. A man of the same age and weight would require 2000 calories a day.

Activity level also has a significant impact on a patient's energy needs. A bedridden patient will obviously expend fewer calories and thus will need to eat fewer. An elderly, bedridden women can need as little as 8.5 calories per pound of body weight: if such a patient weighed 135 pounds, she would need only 1150 calories a day. However, many patients, bedridden or otherwise, have hidden energy needs. The process of healing can be extremely energy intensive—even an immobile patient can use up vast reserves of calories as her body fights infection, knits a fracture, or heals bed sores. Patients on a low-energy diet may also develop deficiencies in micronutrients if the quality of their meals is not monitored closely.

33. According to the passage, which of the patients described below would likely need to consume the most calories per day?

   A) an elderly man on bed rest

   B) a young, overweight man undergoing physical therapy for a broken leg

   C) an elderly man with chronic bed sores

   D) a young, underweight man recovering from a respiratory infection

34. Which of the following is NOT a detail stated in the passage?

   A) A thirty-five-year-old woman who weighs 135 pounds would require at least 2000 calories a day.

   B) Patients' energy needs vary directly with weight and inversely with age.

   C) Carbohydrates, fats, and proteins are macronutrients.

   D) An elderly, bedridden female patient can require as little as 8.5 calories per pound of body weight.

35. What is the meaning of the word *hidden* in the last paragraph?

   A) intentionally kept out of sight

   B) not obvious to the casual observer

   C) easily forgotten

   D) masked by outside complications

36. What is the main idea of the passage?

   A) Patients' diets should include a balance of macro- and micronutrients.

   B) Health care workers can determine how many calories patients need by looking at their weight, age, and activity level.

   C) Meeting the nutritional needs of patients is a complicated but vital responsibility of health care workers.

   D) Activity level of patients should be monitored closely to ensure that each patient receives the amount of macronutrients he or she requires to heal properly.

37. Which of the following is NOT a fact stated in the passage?

   A) Patients require energy from carbohydrates, fats, and proteins as well as essential vitamins and elements to heal properly.

   B) A bedridden patient may require extra calories to provide the body with energy to fuel the healing process.

   C) A poor diet can delay healing in patients.

   D) Female patients should receive fewer calories than male patients so that they don't gain weight.

De Tocqueville's Democracy in America

The following passage contains an excerpt from Alexis de Tocqueville's Democracy in America, *1835*

Alexis de Tocqueville, a young Frenchman from an aristocratic family, visited the United States in the early 1800s. He observed: "Amongst the novel objects that attracted my attention during my stay in the United States, nothing struck me more forcibly than the general equality of conditions. [...] The more I advanced in the study of American society, the more I perceived that the equality of conditions is the fundamental fact from which all others seem to be derived, and the central point at which all my observations constantly terminated."

38. Which of the following best states the main idea of the passage?

A) Alexis de Tocqueville has contributed substantially to the study of the nineteenth-century United States.

B) Equality was the most important ideal in the nineteenth-century United States.

C) In nineteenth-century American society, all people had rights.

D) American society during the nineteenth century was more equal than French society.

39. Based on the context, which of the following is the meaning of the word *novel* in the passage?

A) new

B) written

C) uncertain

D) book

40. The author would most likely agree with which of the following statements about the United States in the nineteenth century?

A) Right from the beginning at least three social classes emerged, with most people falling in the middle.

B) American people were by nature competitive and individualistic.

C) Since the birth of the United States, its citizens have been eager to achieve and prosper.

D) In the early decades when America had just become an independent country with a new government, people lived in equality.

LISTENING

Please visit https://www.triviumtestprep.com/toefl-listening to listen to the recorded lectures for the practice tests.

Dialogue

DIRECTIONS: Listen to the dialogue, then answer the questions.

A new student, Gavin, is speaking with an upperclassman, Leila, about the different types of English classes available at the university.

1. What does Leila think about the poetry classes?

   A) Leila did not take any poetry classes.

   B) Leila thought the poetry classes were too hard.

   C) Leila enjoyed poetry classes.

   D) Leila found the poetry classes too easy.

2. How does Leila feel about classes in literary criticism?

   A) Leila enjoyed them but felt they were difficult.

   B) Leila did not like them because they were too hard.

   C) Leila found them easy and fun.

   D) Leila thought they were too easy and so she did not like them.

3. What do the students think of *Basic Rhetoric and Composition*?

   A) Gavin is taking *Basic Rhetoric and Composition*.

   B) Leila does not recommend *Basic Rhetoric and Composition*.

   C) Both students are taking *Basic Rhetoric and Composition*.

   D) They are disappointed that *Basic Rhetoric and Composition* will not be offered.

4. Who teaches *Basic Rhetoric and Composition*?

   A) Dr. Peters

   B) Dr. Summers

   C) a TA

   D) The students do not know who teaches this class.

5. What do the students discuss about *Creative Writing*?

   A) Leila suggests that Gavin takes *Creative Writing*, and he responds enthusiastically.

   B) Gavin does not like to write creatively, so Leila suggests he choose *Technical Writing* instead.

   C) Leila asks if Gavin recommends *Creative Writing* because he has taken it before.

   D) Gavin expresses interest in *Creative Writing*, but Leila does not know anything about it.

6. How does Gavin feel about the *Shakespearean Media* class?

   A) Gavin is excited to take the class because he enjoys Shakespeare.

   B) Gavin does not like films, so he does not plan to take the class.

   C) Gavin hopes to take the class, but he worries it is full.

   D) Gavin has heard that the class is very difficult.

7. What is Gavin's perspective on *Medieval Vision Literature*?

   A) He thinks it sounds interesting and is enthusiastic about it.

   B) He worries it would be too difficult, so he will not take it.

   C) He has heard that the teacher is a very tough grader.

   D) He is not interested in medieval or Christian topics.

8. Who teaches *Medieval Vision Literature*?

   A) a TA

   B) Dr. Summers

   C) Dr. Peters

   D) The students do not know.

9. Who teaches *Chaucer's Life and Literature*?

   A) Dr. Peters

   B) Dr. Summers

   C) a TA

   D) The students do not know who teaches this class.

10. What do the students think about the class called *Chaucer's Life and Literature*?

    A) Leila thinks that it would be a good class for Gavin to take to improve his English skills.

    B) Leila has taken the class, and the professor wrote her a letter of recommendation for grad school.

    C) Gavin knows the professor, and he explains to Leila that the professor has written him a letter of recommendation.

    D) Gavin has heard of it, and Leila knows students who have taken it to get a letter of recommendation.

Lecture One

DIRECTIONS: Listen to the lecture, then answer the questions.

11. What is the lecture mainly about?

    A) the limits of photosynthesis

    B) the evolution of carnivorous plants

    C) the way to care for carnivorous plants

    D) the struggle that plants undergo to obtain energy

12. According to the professor, why are carnivorous plants still classified as plants?

    A) They get nutrients from the soil.

    B) They lack the ability to move.

    C) They use less chemical energy than animals.

    D) They convert light energy to chemical energy.

13. What does the professor say we have to comprehend before we can understand why plants turn to carnivory?

    A) why plants are unable to move

    B) how photosynthesis works

    C) why any organism evolves

    D) how benefits outweigh costs

14. What is a cost associated with carnivory in plants?

    A) expending energy on luring and catching prey

    B) using up all the available nutrients in the soil

    C) failing to convert light to chemical energy

    D) harming the soil in which they are located

15. What can be inferred about soil based on the lecture?

    A) Plants don't need soil at all to survive.

    B) Carnivorous plants grow more rapidly in dry soil.

    C) Wet soil contains fewer nutrients than plants need.

    D) Most habitats contain soil without nitrogen.

16. Why do plants develop carnivory only in certain habitats?

    A) Many ecosystems lack prey for plants.

    B) Costs and benefits must be weighed.

    C) Some species are more competitive.

    D) Each plant has different energy needs.

17. Why does the professor mention the total number of plant species?

    A) to illustrate the importance of plants in our world

    B) to explain the need to conserve rare plant species

    C) to suggest that many plant species remain undiscovered

    D) to emphasize the rarity of carnivorous plants

18. According to the professor, why would a plant give up carnivory?

    A) Enough sunlight exists for photosynthesis to be successful.

    B) Other plants begin to compete with the plant for resources.

    C) The plant is able to get the nutrients it needs in other ways.

    D) A device to lure and trap prey becomes ineffective.

19. Why do carnivorous plants thrive in environments without a lot of other plants?

    A) They aren't very competitive with other plants.

    B) Other plants compete with them for sunlight.

    C) They have very complex root systems.

    D) Other plants compete with them for prey.

20. What can be inferred when the professor asks, "Does this remind you of anything in the animal kingdom?"

    A) Similarities between plants and animals are quite rare.

    B) Students are better able to understand animals than plants.

    C) Animals also sometimes change their diet based on conditions.

    D) Plants are unique in behavior among most other living organisms.

Lecture Two

DIRECTIONS: Listen to the lecture, then answer the questions.

21. What is the main purpose of the lecture?

    A) to explain how humans have mastered their environment

    B) to trace the history of eating utensils in human history

    C) to suggest that silverware improved human health

    D) to show how human dietary habits have changed over time

22. What was a disadvantage of eating only with the use of human hands?

    A) conflicts at mealtimes

    B) a divide between rich and poor

    C) decaying of natural objects

    D) spread of disease

23. Why were spoons the first specific silverware item?

    A) They were naturally found objects.

    B) They were the most useful utensils.

    C) They allowed humans to lift food out of boiling water.

    D) They helped distinguish between rich and poor.

24. Wealthy individuals in Europe begin to use spoons made of which material?

    A) shell

    B) wood

    C) metal

    D) gourds

25. According to the professor, where were forks first recorded in use?

    A) Egypt

    B) France

    C) Greece

    D) the Middle East

26. What improvement was made to early European forks?

    A) New materials were used.

    B) Points were removed.

    C) New types were created.

    D) Additional tines were added.

27. Why does the professor mention King Louis XIV of France?

    A) He was important in bringing the fork to Europe.

    B) He was one of the first to use a spoon at mealtime.

    C) He helped encourage people to use knives at meals.

    D) He helped end the use of knives with pointed tips.

28. During what time period did a variety of different forks, spoons, and knives begin to be used?

    A) around 400 CE

    B) around 1700 CE

    C) around 1850 CE

    D) around 1000 BCE

29. Why does the professor describe today's knives as being "harmless, dull dinner knives"?

    A) to illustrate that today's knives don't work well

    B) to highlight that dinner knives were once also weapons

    C) to explain that knives are the least important utensils

    D) to show how knives have changed little over time

30. What can be inferred about the professor when she says, "We humans have indeed come a long way from sitting around an open fire and using our hands to serve and eat our food"?

    A) She believes humans still have more to accomplish.

    B) She sees silverware as the greatest human invention.

    C) She believes humans' use of silverware is an accomplishment.

    D) She sees utensils as one way that humans differ from animals.

WRITING

There are two tasks on the Writing test. For the first task, you must read a passage and listen to a lecture on a certain subject. Then write a response answering a question based on what you read and heard.

On the second task, you will respond to a question drawing on your own knowledge and opinions.

Writing Based on Reading and Listening

DIRECTIONS: Read the text below. Then, visit https://www.triviumtestprep.com/toefl-listening. Scroll down to find the relevant recording, and click to listen to the accompanying lecture. You may take notes on the lecture.

Summarize the points made in the lecture, being sure to explain how they respond to specific points made in the reading passage. You will have twenty minutes to write your response. A typical response should be about 150 – 225 words long.

SHAKESPEARE: MAN, NOT MYTH

Was Shakespeare real? This question continues to be a hot-button issue for scholars all over the world. Luckily, the historical record is quite clear when it comes to the existence of the Elizabethan playwright and poet who wrote some of the most beloved literature of the English language.

First of all, there was certainly a man named William Shakespeare. Historical evidence left behind is impossible to refute. We know that he married a woman named Anne Hathaway, thanks to the surviving marriage certificate. We also know he died and left a three-page will dated March 25, 1616. In it, he disposes of his assets primarily to his children, leaving his wife only his "second best bed with furniture." We also have two other documents with his signature, which have been rigorously studied by scholars and found to be authentic.

Some people, of course, believe that a man named William Shakespeare existed. But they argue that this man did not in fact write the plays and poems attributed to him. This is problematic for several reasons. First, most plays of the time period didn't ascribe authorship to any individual. They simply listed the publisher and company of performers. Why then, would someone want to *add* a name to a play when the practice wasn't common? Most likely, because he was a famous playwright. Putting his name on the plays he wrote, which were of high quality, would help encourage people to visit the theater.

Also, other writers of the time knew William Shakespeare. He was a member of the "inner circle" of Renaissance writers. The most notable example is his friendship with Ben Jonson, another poet and playwright. Jonson, who is firmly believed to have existed and been the author of many significant works, wrote about his relationship with Shakespeare and his writings in several of his own pieces. Would he have written about a man who existed only as a pseudonym?

Independent Writing

DIRECTIONS: Read the following prompt. Then, write an essay responding to the question. Use your own experience, ideas, and opinions to develop your response.

You have thirty minutes to plan, write, and revise your essay.

URBAN GROWTH AND CLIMATE CHANGE

Rapid economic growth is not at odds with smart urban development. Some of the most important economic and natural resources of the world are located in areas vulnerable to storms and flooding;

however, with the right planning and investment, economic growth can continue safely and afford-ably.

Can cities grow in areas threatened by climate change, flooding, and storms?

In your essay, take a position on this question. Give reasons for your answer and include any relevant examples from your own knowledge or experience.

ANSWER KEY

READING

1.

Regional Studies	a comparison of the ecosystems of the Great Lakes in the Midwest
Topical Studies	scholarship on the global impact of ozone layer depletion
Physical Studies	a study of volcanoes and volcanic rock
Human Studies	research on the impact of agriculture on prairie habitats

2. **B) is correct.** Only this choice summarizes the two main points of the passage: the definition of geography and the breakdown of its sub-disciplines.

3. **D) is correct.** The passage describes human studies as the study of "the relationship between human activity and the environment," which would include farmers interacting with river systems.

4. **A) is correct.** The passage explains what the study of geography involves and outlines its main sub-disciplines.

5. **B) is correct.** The author writes, "All other explanations for the war are either a direct consequence of the South's desire for wealth at the expense of her fellow man or a fanci-ful invention to cover up this sad portion of our nation's history."

6. **B) is correct.** The author writes, "The Civil War was not a battle of cultural identities—it was a battle about slavery. All other explanations for the war are either a direct consequence of the South's desire for wealth at the expense of her fellow man or a fanciful invention to cover up this sad portion of our nation's history."

7. **A) is correct.** The author writes, "But people who try to sell you this narrative are wrong. The Civil War was not a battle of cultural identities—it was a battle about slavery."

8. **A) is correct.** The bulk of the passage is dedicated to showing that conventional wisdom about "fewer calories in than calories out" isn't true for many people and is more complicated than previously believed.

9. **C) is correct.** The author cites several scientific studies to support the argument.

10. **D) is correct.** People misreporting the amount of food they ate would introduce error into studies on weight loss and might make the studies the author cites unreliable.

11. **D) is correct.** The passage provides the results of a study about the effects of a large-scale nuclear detonation on the ozone layer and a summary of the effects of the Castle/Bravo detonation.

12. **A) is correct.** The Arms Control and Disarmament Agency is working toward that goal.

13. **B) is correct.** Instead of saying "nuclear war," the strategists use the term *exchange*. This is dehumanizing because it minimizes the horrific suffering and devastation to human life that would be caused by large-scale detonations.

14. **B) is correct.** The author presents fact after fact of the dire consequences and serious threat of nuclear detonations, creating the cumulative effect of an urgent warning.

15. **D) is correct.** First, the results of the study conducted by the National Academy of Science are explained; then, the discoveries from a study of the results of the 1954 nuclear detonation are detailed.

16. **A) is correct.** The passage states, "More than any other event in the decade of testing large nuclear weapons in the atmosphere, Castle/Bravo's unexpected contamination of 7,000 square miles of the Pacific Ocean dramatically illustrated how large-scale nuclear war could produce casualties on a colossal scale."

17. **D) is correct.** The consequences of such a detonation were not considered before the detonation and should not be minimized.

18. **D) is correct.** To develop is to gradually advance, which fits the context.

19. **A) is correct.** The status is that testing has stopped, as far as we know; much is known about the technology, but an understanding of the consequences is only developing.

20. **C) is correct.** Global changes are the result of large-scale detonations, according to the study by the Academy of Sciences. The writer states that "reduced ozone concentra-

tions would have a number of consequences outside the areas in which the detonations occurred," and "the increased ultraviolet radiation could also be accompanied by a drop in the average temperature." Overall, "the possibility of a serious increase in ultraviolet radiation has been added to widespread radioactive fallout as a fearsome consequence of the large-scale use of nuclear weapons."

21. **A) is correct.** This choice addresses all of the main ideas of the passage: the flu is potentially deadly, highly infectious, and difficult to contain due to viral shedding.

22. **D) is correct.** According to the passage, "the flu is...relatively difficult to contract," and "while many people who contract the virus will recover, many others will not."

23. **C) is correct.** The second paragraph states that the flu is "relatively difficult to contract" because it "can only be transmitted when individuals come into direct contact with bodily fluids of people infected with the flu or when they are exposed to expelled aerosol particles[.]"

24. **A) is correct.** The author uses the term *measures* to describe the steps that people to take to prevent the spreading of the influenza virus.

25. **C) is correct.** The final paragraph of the passage states that viral shedding is "the process by which the body releases viruses that have been successfully reproducing during the infection."

26. **A) is correct.** The second paragraph of the passage states that "the virus can be contained with fairly simple health measures like hand washing and face masks."

27. **B) is correct.** The author writes that "as these communities have evolved, the species in them have developed complex, long-term interspecies interactions known as symbiotic relationships." She then goes on to describe the different types of symbiotic relationships that exist.

28. **D) is correct.** The author writes, "Often, relationships described as commensal include one species that feeds on another species' leftovers; remoras, for instance, will attach themselves to sharks and eat the food particles they leave behind. It might seem like the shark gets nothing from the relationship, but a closer look will show that sharks in fact benefit from remoras, which clean the sharks' skin and remove parasites."

29. **C) is correct.** The author writes, "A relationship where one individual benefits and the other is harmed is known as parasitism."

30. **A) is correct.** The author writes, "But is it possible for two species to interact and for one to remain completely unaffected?...In fact, many scientists claim that relationships currently described as commensal are just mutualistic or parasitic in ways that haven't been discovered yet."

31. **A) is correct.** The author writes that "there's another class of symbiosis that is controversial among scientists" and goes on to say that "many scientists claim the relationships currently described as commensal are just mutualistic or parasitic in ways that haven't been discovered yet." This implies that scientists debate about the topic of commensalism.

32. **D) is correct.** The author writes, "The bacteria, fungi, insects, plants, and animals that live together in a habitat have evolved to share a pool of limited resources...As these communities have evolved, the species in them have developed complex, long-term interspecies interactions known as symbiotic relationships."

33. **B) is correct.** The author writes that "generally, energy needs are directly related to a person's weight and inversely related to age; it's also generally true that men require more calories than women." Additionally, she points out that "the process of healing can be extremely energy intensive."

34. **A) is correct.** The author writes, "Thus, a thirty-five-year-old woman who weighs 135 pounds will require around 1800 calories a day."

35. **B) is correct.** The author writes, "However, many patients, bedridden or otherwise, have hidden energy needs. The process of healing can be extremely energy intensive—even an immobile patient can use up vast reserves of calories as her body fights infection, knits a fracture, or heals bed sores." While a bedridden patient's activity levels may be low, he or she is consuming energy at a high rate while healing.

36. **C) is correct.** The author opens the passage saying, "Because the needs of every patient will be different, it's the task of every health care facility to ensure that patients receive the proper nutrition." He then goes on to detail some of the factors that determine each patients' unique needs and describes some of the effects of proper and poor nutrition.

37. **D) is correct.** The author writes, "Generally, energy needs are directly related to a person's weight and inversely related to age; it's also generally true that men require more calories than women." However, he does not relate calorie needs to weight gain.

38. **B) is correct.** The author notes de Tocqueville's observation: "The more I advanced in the study of American society, the more I perceived that the equality of conditions is the fundamental fact from which all others seem to be derived," implying that equality was the most important ideal in the United States. However, de Tocqueville does not account for Native Americans, enslaved people of African descent, or women.

39. **A) is correct.** *New* best describes the idea that the writer is encountering things he has never seen before.

40. **D) is correct.** "Equality of conditions" suggests that people's living conditions, in terms of economics and social status, were equal. (Notably, de Tocqueville does not mention enslaved people of African descent, Native Americans, or women.)

Dialogue

A new student, Gavin, is speaking with an upperclassman, Leila, about the different types of English classes available at the university.

Leila: Go ahead and ask me anything. I'm in my last semester as an English major. I've probably taken most of these classes.

Gavin: There are just so many classes. I never know which ones are best for me. Which kinds of English classes were your favorite?

Leila: I liked the poetry classes, especially the one about English Romantic poets. Those were pretty straightforward, and as long as I went to class and did the reading, I did well in those. I also liked the classes in literary criticism, but they are quite hard. You have to really know your stuff to get an A.

Gavin: What about writing classes?

Leila: Well, there is *Basic Rhetoric and Composition*—not sure who's teaching that this year. It's pretty simple, and I'm sure you've already registered for that. Then there's *Technical Writing* with Dr. Peters. I'd really recommend you take that since I learned a lot in that class. There's *Creative Writing* as well, also taught by Dr. Peters. It's a great class, especially if you enjoy reading your work out loud.

Gavin: I've registered for *Rhetoric and Comp*...Writing is one of my hobbies, so those classes sound great! I saw a class called *Shakespearean Media* that I can take as a freshman. I also saw some other classes with interesting titles, like *Medieval Vision Literature* and *Chaucer's Life and Literature*.

Leila: The Shakespeare class focuses on the way the plays have been contextualized in modern media, such as film. That's a great class to take if you like watching movies!

Gavin: I'm not a big movie fan. I probably won't take that.

Leila: *Medieval Vision Literature* is also taught by Dr. Peters. It contains a lot of allusions to Catholic Christianity and is really interesting.

Gavin: That sounds awesome!

Leila: The class on Chaucer is taught by Dr. Summers, Chair of the English department. I've never taken it personally, but I have friends who've told me that it is a good class to take if you want to get a letter of recommendation for grad school. Dr. Summers writes many of those.

1. **C) is correct.** Leila says, "I liked the poetry classes, especially the one about English Romantic poets."

2. **A) is correct.** Leila says, "I also liked the classes in literary criticism, but they are quite hard. You have to really know your stuff to get an A."

3. **A) is correct.** Gavin says, "I've registered for *Rhetoric and Comp*." Leila only discusses it as an option, saying, "Well, there is *Basic Rhetoric and Composition*—not sure who's teaching that this year."

4. **C) is correct.** Leila says, "Well, there is *Basic Rhetoric and Composition*—not sure who's teaching that this year."

5. **A) is correct.** According to Leila, "There's *Creative Writing* as well, also taught by Dr. Peters. It's a great class, especially if you

enjoy reading your work out loud. Gavin says, "Writing is one of my hobbies, so those classes sound great!"

6. **B) is correct.** Leila explains, "The Shake-speare class focuses on the way the plays have been contextualized in modern media, such as film. That's a great class to take if you like watching movies!" Gavin responds, "I'm not a big movie fan. I probably won't take that."

7. **A) is correct.** When Leila describes *Medieval Vision Literature*, Gavin replies, "That sounds awesome!"

8. **C) is correct.** Leila says, "*Medieval Vision Literature* is also taught by Dr. Peters."

9. **B) is correct.** Leila says, "The class on Chaucer is taught by Dr. Summers."

10. **D) is correct.** Gavin says, "I also saw some other classes with interesting titles, like *Medieval Vision Literature* and *Chaucer's Life and Literature*." Leila adds that the "class on Chaucer is taught by Dr. Summers, Chair of the English department. I've never taken it personally, but I have friends who've told me that it is a good class to take if you want to get a letter of recommendation for grad school."

Lecture One

I want to start by reminding everyone of the fundamental difference between a plant and an animal. While there are many differences, the most basic understanding is that plants make their own food whereas animals must eat something else to survive. But is this always the case? Have you heard of carnivorous plants?

Hopefully you have. Probably the most famous one is the Venus flytrap, which snaps closed to consume its prey. So, are these organisms plants or animals? And do they still use photosynthesis?

These carnivorous plants are a little more complex than most plants, but they are certainly still plants. It is important to remember that they get some nutrients from eating other organisms, but they *still* use photosynthesis. Do you remember what photosynthesis is?

Yes. It's the process in which plants convert light energy to chemical energy that they can use as fuel.

The real question is not whether these are plants but why and how certain plants evolved to have such capabilities that allow them to eat other organisms. To understand this, we first have to understand why any organism would evolve or change. They do this because it makes sense. A need for a new approach exists, and the benefits of the new approach outweigh the costs.

One reason a plant might need a different approach might be because the plant lives in soil that doesn't provide enough important nutrients, like nitrogen. Since we know that a plant can't simply get up and move to a new patch of soil with better nutrients, it has to find another way to get what it needs.

Carnivory, though, takes a lot of energy. While plants aren't chasing after their prey like a cheetah or a lion, they still have to lure and trap it. This takes effort. Returning to the cost/benefit approach then, the payoff has to make sense for the plant. If too much energy is used to try to obtain prey, then the adaptation wouldn't be worth it.

Studies show that the energy required to build and manage a device to catch prey, like a lure and a mechanism that snaps shut when the prey lands, is pretty high. That means that plants that *can* get all the nutrients they need from the soil do not invest in such an adaptation. Only plants in very inhospitable habitats where the soil can't give them all the nutrients they need—like bogs, marshes, and swamps—develop the capability to eat other organisms.

This makes carnivorous plants pretty rare. There are only around 580 such species. This isn't a very big chunk of the 391,000 species of plants on planet Earth. These special plants also only grow in very particular habitats. They tend to prefer moist soil and humidity and don't grow at a rapid rate, so they aren't very competitive with other plants nearby. So they are typically found in habitats where other plants would not thrive.

Furthermore, not all carnivorous plants use their capabilities at all times. Some stop eating prey when they can get the nutrients they need to survive in other ways or when the energy expended on carnivory exceeds the benefits. Does this remind you of anything in the animal kingdom?

11. **B) is correct.** According to the professor, "The real question is not whether these are plants but why and how certain plants evolved to have such capabilities that allow them to eat other organisms." The central idea of the lecture is how and why certain plants evolved to become carnivorous.

12. **D) is correct.** According to the professor, these plants "still use photosynthesis," which is "the process in which plants convert light energy to chemical energy that they can use as fuel."

13. **C) is correct.** The professor says, "The real question is not whether these are plants but why and how certain plants evolved to have such capabilities that allow them to eat other organisms. To understand this, we first have to understand why any organism would evolve or change."

14. **A) is correct.** The professor states, "Carnivory, though, takes a lot of energy. While plants aren't chasing after their prey like a cheetah or a lion, they still have to lure and trap it. This takes effort."

15. **C) is correct.** According to the professor, "bogs, marshes, and swamps" are "very inhospitable habitats where the soil can't give [plants] all the nutrients they need." The most logical conclusion is that wet soil contains fewer nutrients since these are all damp/wet environments.

16. **B) is correct.** The professor states, "Returning to the cost/benefit approach then, the payoff has to make sense for the plant. If too much energy is used to try to obtain prey, then the adaptation wouldn't be worth it."

17. **D) is correct.** The professor compares the number of carnivorous plants to the total number of plants to show their rarity: "This makes carnivorous plants pretty rare. There are only around 580 such species. This isn't a very big chunk of the 391,000 species of plants on planet Earth."

18. **C) is correct.** The professor explains, "not all carnivorous plants use their capabilities at all times. Some stop eating prey when they can get the nutrients they need to survive in other ways or when the energy expended on carnivory exceeds the benefits."

19. **A) is correct.** The professor states, "They tend to prefer moist soil and humidity and don't grow at a rapid rate, so they aren't very competitive with other plants nearby. So they are typically found in habitats where other plants would not thrive."

20. **C) is correct.** This is a logical inference for the context (a biology class). The class might know about similar adaptations that animals make, such as changing their diet depending upon what food is available.

Lecture Two

Let's talk a little bit about how humans have interacted with and "mastered" their environment. We learned last time that humans began to cook food because doing so allowed them to consume more nutrients. However, the *way* that humans eat their food has also changed over time. For a lot of human history, the fingers were the primary utensils used to eat with. There were disadvantages to this. Some food dropped to the ground, and since hands weren't always clean, people sometimes spread disease while eating. This changed with a better method for eating—using silverware. But like other human inventions, silverware started out slowly and changed over time.

Spoons were the first type of silverware to make their way to the human table. If you think about it, this is logical because many natural objects, like shells or dried gourds, are natural scooping mechanisms. It is not known when natural objects first began being used as spoons, but human-fashioned spoons were known to exist from 1000 BCE in Egypt.

As spoons spread throughout the world, they also became a way to distinguish between the wealthy and the not-so-wealthy. Historical records suggest that in Europe, wooden spoons were used by most individuals, and only the wealthiest individuals had spoons made of metal.

The fork has a slightly more interesting past. While prehistoric people likely used forked twigs and branches for a variety of purposes, the first recorded use of forks was in ancient Greece. These forks weren't used by individuals though. They were used to get food—primarily meat—out of boiling water safely. It was quite some time before forks became part of every meal. Historians date the dinner fork to around 400 CE in the Middle East.

It took a while for the fork to become a global phenomenon. It wasn't until the early eleventh century CE that the fork made its way to Europe. Even then, forks were most often reserved only for messy foods. As time passed, many Europeans began to see the benefits of forks; however, because they had only two or three tines, food was still known to slip off. Luckily, in the early 1700s, a fourth tine was added to the fork, and the new, more effective utensil became commonplace on many tables.

Knives have also been around for a very long time—they were what the earliest humans used to catch their food! Early knives were very sharp and typically brought to the table by the owner. Sometimes they were used as a device to clean one's teeth or even to threaten others at the meal!

As you can imagine, this wasn't always an ideal situation, especially in contentious times. To lower the chance of mealtime brawls, King Louis XIV decreed an end to pointed knives in France. This trend of blunt-ended knives quickly moved beyond France and is responsible for the harmless, dull dinner knives we have today.

People also began to customize silverware. By the middle of the nineteenth century, many tables in the Western world had a variety of different forks, spoons, and knives: for salads, fish, desserts, soup, tea, steak, and more. Proper dining etiquette or "table manners" also became important in certain social circles. Eating, which was once primarily done solely with one's fingers, became quite a production. Today's tables, particularly those set for fine dining, often have silverware for every imaginable situation, from buttering bread to stirring iced tea. We humans have indeed come a long way from sitting around an open fire and using our hands to serve and eat our food.

21. **B) is correct.** This lecture explains the history of silverware. The professor states, "like other human inventions, silverware started out slowly and changed over time."

22. **D) is correct.** The professor states that the spread of disease was one major disadvantage: "Some food dropped to the ground, and since hands weren't always clean, people sometimes spread disease while eating."

23. **A) is correct.** The lecture tells us that it made sense for spoons to be the first specific silverware item "because many natural objects, like shells or dried gourds, are natural scooping mechanisms."

24. **C) is correct.** According to the professor, "Historical records suggest that in Europe, wooden spoons were used by most individuals, and only the wealthiest individuals had spoons made of metal."

25. **C) is correct.** The professor states, "While prehistoric people likely used forked twigs and branches for a variety of purposes, the first recorded use of forks was in ancient Greece."

26. **D) is correct.** The professor explains that early forks needed improvement because food still slipped off: "Luckily, in the early 1700s, a fourth tine was added to the fork, and the new, more effective utensil became commonplace on many tables."

27. **D) is correct.** The professor explains, "King Louis XIV decreed an end to pointed knives in France."

28. **C) is correct.** The year 1850 CE is the "middle of the nineteenth century," which is stated in the lecture as when these different types of silverware came into use.

29. **B) is correct.** This helps remind readers that at one time knives were sometimes used "even to threaten others at the meal!" This is what prompted King Louis XIV to outlaw sharp knives at the table.

30. **C) is correct.** When someone has "come a long way," this means that someone has made a significant accomplishment. Though humans once used only their hands to eat and fought at the table, now they have many more choices.

WRITING

Who was William Shakespeare? Was there such a man? Did he write all those plays? How can one man possess so much genius? Scholars have every reason to ask these questions. Many believe that the man referred to as William Shakespeare did not actually write the many works ascribed to him, and for good reason.

The strongest evidence that Shakespeare did not write the works attributed to him is his lack of formal education. That sharply contrasts with his seemingly flawless command of the English language—not to mention the many important cultural references included in his works. These references likely would not have been known to someone without higher education.

Most historians believe that even though Shakespeare attended grammar school, his schooling likely ended around age fourteen. There is no record of his education beyond this period. It remains quite unlikely that a man without a high school education could have penned such masterpieces.

Who then wrote these pieces and why not take credit for them? Well, the answer might lie in the social mores of Elizabethan England. You see, working as a writer lacked the prestige it has today. The aristocrats of the time, even if they enjoyed artistic expression, often wrote under pseudonyms to protect their reputations.

The person or persons who authored the works attributed to Shakespeare also had to protect their identities for another reason: the works were sometimes critical of the British government and monarchy. While freedom of speech is something we hold in high regard today, no such freedoms were guaranteed in Elizabethan England. Open criticism of the government could be seen as treason and could be punished by death.

All of this leads me—and will hopefully lead you—to believe that the author of these works was actually Sir Francis Bacon, Viscount of St. Albans. Francis Bacon, born in 1561, was, unlike William Shakespeare, a true Renaissance man who studied at Cambridge, traveled the globe, invented the scientific method, and wrote seminal works in philosophy.

And why Bacon would have wanted to conceal his identity has already been established. He was a nobleman and a scholar, not a lowly writer of plays. Furthermore, he was a secret critic of the government of the time. He is believed to have collaborated with other like-minded men, like Sir Walter Raleigh, a famed explorer, to pen subversive literature—very much like some of the works that are ascribed to a man named Shakespeare.

Consider Shakespeare's most famous works: *Macbeth*, *Hamlet*, *Richard III*. These plays portray monarchs as ruthless, power-hungry individuals willing to lie, cheat, and even murder to get what they want. They are a vicious critique of the ruling class.

So, is William Shakespeare the author of the thirty-seven plays attributed to him? Not very likely. What about the poetry also attributed to him? I have a theory on the true author of those as well, but we will have to save that for next class.

Writing Based on Reading and Listening: Sample Student Response

Summarize the points made in the lecture, being sure to explain how they respond to specific points made in the reading passage.

The lecture establishes that Sir Francis Bacon was the true author of Shakespeare's plays. Shakespeare, according to the lecture, could not have written the works because he had a lack of education and attended school only to age fourteen. On the other hand, the text points to the wealth of historical evidence that shows of the existence of a man named William Shakespeare.

While the text talks about the importance of Shakespeare being listed as the author in a time when many plays did not list authors, the lecture states that Shakespeare was only a pen name of Sir Francis Bacon. He could not write under his real name because of his high social standing and because the plays were somewhat critical of government.

The lecture sees Bacon, a highly educated world traveler, as much more able to have written such works than Shakespeare. Though the text mentions that other writers of the time, such as Ben Jonson, knew and wrote about Shakespeare the man, the lecture maintains that it is more likely Bacon was actually Shakespeare. He simply couldn't sign his own name to such works because it would not have been fitting of his role as a gentleman.

Independent Writing: Sample Student Response

Recent powerful storms have caused extreme destruction, especially in cities and areas where population has been growing rapidly. But these growing centers of population power the national economies of global industrial powers. We cannot just abandon cities where hurricanes, cyclones, and typhoons strike. Economic development and growth can continue. Governments can secure communities using lessons learned from past tragedies. The solution is to encourage investment in urban planning and public safety.

Before growing cities get even larger, governments must take action to prevent the growth of slums, improve existing infrastructure for cities (or develop new infrastructure), and establish good urban management policies. In addition, the private sector can sponsor urban development and safety.

In the United States, the Gulf Coast area contains oil and gas resources and major ports. Securing the coastal areas is a smart investment. Farther north, New York City and its region are an important part of the world economy. Both areas are central to global markets and vulnerable to storms and flooding. Slowing any growth in these areas would damage the global financial and fossil fuel markets.

Fast-growing South and Southeast Asia—the Philippines, Bangladesh, Myanmar, Vietnam, Malaysia, and Indonesia—are vulnerable to storms. So are Taiwan, Hong Kong, and parts of India. These places are also home to the factories and workers who produce many of the world's consumer products. Slowing development would hurt these countries. Millions of people would lose jobs and opportunities.

Today, there are more ways than ever to develop products and procedures to ensure safety. Cities can establish evacuation routes and procedures. NGOs can distribute survival items during storm seasons. Technology can warn residents about dangerous conditions, giving them time to prepare and making it possible to live in storm-prone areas more safely.

While storms and other natural disasters will remain a threat to human life, we cannot stop all economic activity. Thanks to cooperation and innovation, countries can protect communities as they drive the economic growth of those regions affected by major storms. That way, development can continue in as safe an environment as possible.

www.ingramcontent.com/pod-product-compliance
Lightning Source LLC
Chambersburg PA
CBHW062051090426
42740CB00016B/3101